Chesapeake Men

Chesapeake Men

Their Stories ✦ Their Memories

Don Parks

Terry —
Enjoy the book.

Don Parks

Schiffer Publishing Ltd

4880 Lower Valley Road • Atglen, PA 19310

Other Schiffer Books on Related Subjects:

Dancing With the Tide: Watermen of the Chesapeake,
978-0-8703-3532-7, $24.95
Voices of the Chesapeake Bay, 978-0-9787-2788-8, $29.95
Yesterday on the Chesapeake Bay, 978-0-7643-2597-7, $39.95

Designed by Molly Shields
Cover Designed by John P. Cheek
Type set in Caslon Old face BT/ New Baskerville BT

ISBN: 978-0-7643-4461-9
Printed in China

Published by Schiffer Publishing, Ltd.
4880 Lower Valley Road
Atglen, PA 19310
Phone: (610) 593-1777; Fax: (610) 593-2002
E-mail: Info@schifferbooks.com

For our complete selection of fine books on this and related subjects,
please visit our website at **www.schifferbooks.com**. You may also
write for a free catalog.

This book may be purchased from the publisher. Please try your
bookstore first.

We are always looking for people to write books on new and
related subjects. If you have an idea for a book, please contact us at
proposals@schifferbooks.com.

Schiffer Publishing's titles are available at special discounts for
bulk purchases for sales promotions or premiums. Special editions,
including personalized covers, corporate imprints, and excerpts can
be created in large quantities for special needs. For more information,
contact the publisher.

To the memory of Loretta Larrimore
and Betty Simpkins

Acknowledgments

My sincere thanks go to the men whose biographies are contained in this book. Their willingness to share their lives in an unselfish and generous manner has been invaluable. These are men who are honest and sincere. They are void of pretense and are straight-forward in their interactions with others. It has been a pleasure getting to know each of them.

In addition to the eleven people whose stories are featured in this book, several others deserve recognition. Appreciation goes to Ed Thieler for suggesting that I include Dallas Bradshaw. Ed also provided the photo of Dallas and his wife Kakie. Thanks to Jack Smith for urging me to include the Honorable Lloyd "Hot Dog" Simpkins. Thanks are also extended to Clarence Marshall for introducing me to Dave McQuay.

Gratitude is extended to my wife, Linda, for her patience and support during the lengthy process of writing, researching, and editing. Finally, thanks to my daughter, Jodi, for her technical expertise and advice in the preparation of the manuscript.

Contents

Introduction

People read for the enjoyment of the story, or stories, contained within the covers of a book. Stories may be educational, entertaining, fascinating, or inspiring. They can be mystical, spiritual, or just plain fun to read. All of these adjectives describe the array of stories contained in this compendium.

You, the readers, will meet eleven unforgettable men who make their homes near the banks of the Chesapeake Bay. The stories these folks collectively convey about life near the largest estuary in the United States will both enlightening and educational. In many ways, this great Bay helped influence their character and made them the men they later became. These men grew up on Maryland's portion of the Eastern Shore.

The magnificent Chesapeake pierced the land mass of the state and separated it east to west. The Bay was a barrier between the two shores. Getting to the Eastern Shore was a chore. Long ferry boat rides were necessary to get to the place. It took a lot of effort to get there. Metropolitan areas flourished on the western portion of the Chesapeake while the Eastern Shore remained sparsely populated and rural.

As a result, the folks in the small towns on the eastern side of the bay developed a lifestyle that was characterized by closeness of community and caring for their fellow citizens. Virtually all native shoremen shared similar beliefs and virtues. Strangers were few in the communities that made up the Shore. This created an insular society that resisted change, a society that was fiercely self-sufficient.

Certain ways of living were unique to these Eastern Shoremen. Much of this was linked to traditions that extended back to the days when their forefathers landed from Anglo-Saxon Europe. Old ways were valued and respected. Expectations from one family to another did not often vary, as these families lived very similar lifestyles.

A great many of these people relied on the Chesapeake for a livelihood. Oysters, crabs, and clams were abundant and the great Bay provided a good income for generations. These were hard-working, industrious people whose lives were closely entwined with the nature by which they were surrounded.

With the coming of the Chesapeake Bay Bridge in 1952, the Eastern Shore lifestyle began to change. The influx of folks from other areas gradually weakened the uniqueness of the Eastern Shore culture. In many parts of the now thickly settled Eastern Shore that uniqueness has all but disappeared.

Simultaneously, the bounty from the Chesapeake began to suffer. No longer were men able to eke out a living from the waters of the Bay as they had in the past. The Chesapeake grew ill from the effects of decades of pollution and mistreatment.

The Eastern Shoremen will adjust to the social changes brought on by urbanization. Only time will tell, however, if the Chesapeake Bay will bounce back to more than a shadow of its former healthy self.

CHAPTER ONE

Dave McQuay

Fiberglass, carbon fiber, and composite are only a few of the production materials used in the manufacture of most of today's boats. Advanced building techniques are required to produce the current assembly-line models that flood the marketplace. In this high-tech age of boat production, Dave McQuay is an anomaly. He designs, builds, and repairs boats the old-fashioned way, primarily from wood. The fourth-generation boat-builder plies his trade in much the same manner as his forefathers.

"My great, great grandfather on my mother's side was Benjamin Harrison," said McQuay. "He was one of the first settlers on Tilghman Island. He moved his family there shortly after the island was first subdivided in the 1840s. He was a farmer, but his son, Joseph L. Harrison, took up the shipbuilding trade. He built bugeyes, schooners, and smaller sailboats called log canoes. He acquired a reputation for building quality boats."

Bugeyes were rigged with two masts and a jib. Like log canoes, Bugeyes were used to dredge for oysters. These boats would sail over the oyster bars dragging iron, cage-like triangular dredges that were tethered to the boat by a cable, scooping up oysters from the bottom of the Bay. Usually, a dredge was pulled on either side of the boat. Later, when engines were installed in boats for propulsion, bugeyes carried push boats, or yawl boats, on davits hung from their sterns (after end of the boat). These boats utilized converted automobile engines for propulsion. When entering and leaving port, push boats acted like tugs, positioning the bugeye as required. Push boats were twelve to fourteen feet in length. In the summer, bugeyes were used to haul cargo around the Bay. A variety of vegetables, fruit, and other commodities were taken to Baltimore and elsewhere on the decks of these vessels.

Constructed similarly to the dugout canoes fashioned by Native Americans, log canoes and bugeyes were hollowed from large diameter logs. Native Americans carefully chipped and burned the interior of the log little by little, leaving a shell that was sharpened on both ends, thus forming a boat. Yankee ingenuity was later utilized and several logs were pinned together and their ends shaped to form larger and wider boats. By the time Joseph L. Harrison was building canoes and bugeyes three, five, seven and nine logs were being joined together. Sprit sails were added and the craft was ready for the rigors of oystering in the cold waters of the Chesapeake.

"Joseph L. Harrison's log canoes were noted for speed and many continue in use today, over one hundred years since they were constructed," said Dave. "Joseph Harrison's son was John B. Harrison, my grandfather. He became more renown than his father. He went on to become one of the best-known designers and builders on the Chesapeake. In his time, there were three top builders in the Bay area: Joseph Brooks from Dorchester County, John Bradford from Fairmount in Somerset County, and my grandfather. He was a master shipwright. He began working with his father when he was twelve years old. He dropped out of school but he had someone tutor him and he went on to learn algebra and other math skills. He was an impressive guy.

"He constructed his first bugeye, the *Mary L. Cooper*, in 1882 when he was only seventeen years old. He and his father were prolific builders; they built a bugeye every year. In 1889, when he was 24, he built the *Edna L. Lockwood*. The nine log *Lockwood*, at 53-1/2 feet overall, is currently on display at the Chesapeake Bay Maritime Museum in St. Michaels. She is the only remaining bugeye in existence still rigged as a sailing vessel.

"The largest boat that Grandfather Harrison built was the *Emma A. Faulkner*. At seventy-two feet on her waterline, she was one of the biggest bugeyes ever built. On deck she measured eighty-two or eighty-three feet in length. Unlike earlier boats, she had a round stern, which aided stability. She was built in 1900 for Capt. Joe Faulkner who named her for his wife. My grandfather had once trained as a blacksmith and he did all the ironwork on the boat including building the dredges. He charged Capt. Joe $2,500 for the completed boat. She was one of the best and fastest bugeyes that ever sailed. In many ways, she was his masterpiece."

McQuay explained that, unlike the early bugeyes, the *Faulkner* was not log-built. "She was built plank on frame like most modern workboats," he said. "She was designated as a 1,500-bushel boat; she was built to haul 1,500 bushels of oysters. Every year, in those days, the *Baltimore Sunpapers* would sponsor a race for workboats. These races were held from 1921 until 1931. The *Faulkner* won the bugeye class four or five years in a row. She retired undefeated.

"Capt. Joe later sold her to a man in Cambridge. She ended her days up on the Wicomico River near Salisbury. She had been in a collision with another boat and broken her mainmast and was abandoned in the shallows at Shad Point about 1949."

Like his bugeyes, Capt. John B. Harrison's log canoes were very well built. "The *Jay Dee* and the *Flying Cloud* are two of his canoes that continue to actively race in the log canoe circuit," Dave said. "He also built many other vessels designed solely to work the waters of the Bay."

Shortly after the Harrison family moved to the island, William Mathias Covington relocated to Tilghman with his family from Wicomico County, Maryland. "He bought waterfront property on the east side of the island and built a shop there at a place known as Devil's Island," Dave explained. "He was a trained shipwright with experience in log-boat construction. In 1856, he launched the first log canoe that was built on the island, the *Kuddle*."

One of Covington's daughters married James Lowery, who had moved to the island after the Civil War. "Lowery learned the boat-building trade from his father-in-law," Dave said. "By the early 1870s, Tilghman Island had become one of three centers for log canoe construction on the Chesapeake Bay. Other major locations were Poquoson, Virginia, and the Pocomoke River, in Somerset County, on Maryland's Eastern Shore. On Tilghman, over forty log canoes and nearly as many bugeyes were built. The Covington's, Harrison's and Lowery's built the majority of canoes that came from Tilghman Island."

William Covington's son, Sidney, continued his father's boat-building tradition. He was a prolific builder of log canoes. Among the canoes he fashioned, several remain in use today. The *Island Bird* (1882) and the *Island Blossom* (1892) actively compete in Chesapeake Bay log canoe races.

The highly respected Talbot County builders of log canoes, Sidney Covington and John B. Harrison have both been immortalized by the Chesapeake Bay Log Canoe Racing Association. There are trophies, named in their honor, awarded during the prestigious Governor's Cup racing series. The Sidney Covington trophy is awarded to the first-place boat built prior to 1917 and the John B. Harrison trophy is awarded to the first-place boat built after 1917.

"Sidney Covington converted the very first log canoe to power in 1900," said Dave. "As the internal combustion engine became more popular for marine usage, about the turn of the twentieth century, many log canoes were converted from sail power to engine power. In 1902, Covington built the first workboat to be powered by a gasoline engine, the 48-foot *Elmira*. He used this boat in his oyster business."

Covington's oyster business was located on a spit of land that jutted out from Tilghman, which would ultimately be known as Avalon Island. "Covington gave the place its name," said McQuay. "There is a housing development there now called Tilghman on the Chesapeake. In addition to the oyster-processing operation, Sidney Covington and his sons ran a store at the same location. There was even a post office there. The post office had a drive up window for mail delivery. When I was a kid, I remember seeing that in operation."

Dave explained that Sidney Covington was married to Mary Jane (Sinclair) Covington. Mary Jane's parents had once been lighthouse keepers on nearby Sharp's Island at the mouth of the Choptank River.

"John B. Harrison, my grandfather, was married twice. His first wife was Amelia Covington, daughter of Sidney Covington. After her death in 1902, he married her sister, Lottie, the following year. Lottie was my mother's mother."

Dave explained that by 1900, bugeyes were being replaced by skipjacks. "Skipjacks appeared largely because of economics," said Dave. "They were much simpler to build and maintain than bugeyes. They were plank on frame construction, making them less expensive to build. Watermen could afford to lay them up (not use them) during the off season rather than run freight with them. By 1910, bugeye production on the Chesapeake had virtually ceased.

"Most skipjacks were generally smaller than bugeyes. Like bugeyes, they had centerboards that enabled them to dredge in shallow water. Skipjacks, though, only have only one mast and a jib sail. However, they work the oyster beds in much the same manner as bugeyes. They also are pushed by yawl boats that rest in davits hung from their stern when not in use.

"Skipjacks originated in Somerset County around the towns of Oriole, Champ, and Mount Vernon. Down there they had sailing boats they called baby bateaus at that time. These boats were sixteen to twenty feet in length. Skipjacks were an enlarged version of baby bateaus. They came on the scene in the mid-1890s."

According to Dave, by the 1880s over nine hundred boats were dredging for oysters in Maryland's portion of the Chesapeake. Additionally, over 6,000 canoes were registered in the state to tong for oysters. Tonging involved using long wooden shafts that were pinned to allow them to be opened and closed in scissor-like fashion in an effort to dislodge oysters from the depths of the Bay. Attached to the ends of the shafts were iron, cage-like appendices in which the oysters were captured.

The state of Maryland, in the mid-1800s, outlawed oyster dredging in steam-powered vessels for fear of depleting the supply of oysters. Only sail-powered vessels were allowed to dredge in Maryland's portion of the Chesapeake. With modifications, the law remains in effect. Thus, the Chesapeake Bay skipjack fleet is the sole commercial sailing fleet remaining in the United States. Today, about a dozen skipjacks remain. Of these, only a handful still dredge for oysters.

"My dad was Sam McQuay," Dave said. "He gave me my middle name, Lesley. I was named after a good friend of his, Lesley Edgecomb, who owned the Edgecomb Steel Co. in Pittsburg. Dad did quite a bit of work on his yacht. Dad was also instrumental in Edgecomb's purchase of property at the head of Tilghman Island, a place known as Black Walnut Point. When I married, Edgecomb gave us a $100 war bond. I still have that bond. I've never cashed it."

After graduation from high school in 1927, Sam McQuay worked in a grocery store and also painted houses. Following the aftermath of the 1933 storm, his father-in-law, Captain John B. Harrison, asked if he would help rebuild his shop, which had suffered lots of damage from the hurricane. "Dad agreed and stayed on and learned the boat-building trade," said Dave. "The two built mostly power boats for local watermen. They also built a number of pleasure boats.

"In 1943, dad went to work for the Navy at the Oxford Boatyard. The yard had a contract to build boats during the war. They built two types of boats there and dad headed up one of the building crews.

"In 1945, my grandfather died. After World War II ended, my grandmother allowed James Lowrey and his son, Maynard, the use of the boat shop on Devil's Island and dad continued to work in Oxford at the Crockett Brothers boat yard. He worked there until 1950.

"Dr. Guy Reeser owned a piece of property on Tilghman Island near the western end of the narrows. He had a desire to do something with the property that was on the waterfront. Dr. Reeser and his friend, Harry Fairbank, were great horse racing fans. They went up to Pimlico and bet a lot of money on a horse named 14 Grand. The horse won the race and they came home and, with their winnings, dug out a marina on Dr. Reeser's property. They also set up a store there. They named their business venture 14 Grand. Dad went into business with them building and repairing boats using the railway they had constructed. Later, he returned to Crockett Bros. for another stint.

"George Jackson was a good friend of dad's and he owned a boat building shop in the town of Wittman; north of Tilghman. The building where his shop was located was moved about one hundred yards to its present location on the waterfront in 1931. In August 1956, he sold the shop to dad for $3,000. In addition to the building, lots of tools and equipment were included in the sale."

Jackson, Dave explained, was well known for building boats that were referred to as pot pie skiffs, or tuck sterns. When Dave's dad bought the shop, Jackson had half dozen orders for potpie skiffs. Ranging from sixteen to forty feet in length, pot pies had a unique after section. Instead of squared off sterns, the rear of pot pie skiffs gently angled upward from the water with a tuck. The V-shaped bottom followed all the way to its end. "This design enabled the boat to push through the water easier," Dave said. "They cut through the water like a sailboat and threw very little wake. These boats could be anchored from the stern without fear of their foundering when they needed to get in a better position for oystering."

After filling those orders, Dave's father turned to building box stern designs (squared off after sections). A number of pleasure boats came out of his shop, some as large as forty-five feet. "Dad built his boats from plans he had drawn himself," Dave said. "He used half models in designing his boats. All of the builders patterned their boats from half models. Half models are built to represent ½ to ¾ of an inch per foot. When I build a boat today, I continue to use the system. Each builder's boats had a unique look. You could usually tell who built a boat just by looking at the way they were designed."

The elder McQuay also built work boats from thirty-six to forty-five feet in length. He also constructed several small sailboats and a Whitehall rowing skiff. According to McQuay, the whitehall is now on display in the Mystic Seaport Museum in Mystic, Connecticut.

"I started helping dad when I was twelve years old when he first opened the shop," Dave stated. "By 1959, I was able to contribute a lot and worked full time during summer vacations." Fully expecting to work side by side with his father following graduation from high school in 1962, Dave's father, instead, steered his son away from the business. "Dad grew up during the depression and knew the value of a pay check," he stated. "Dad insisted that I get a regular job, one that would provide me with a steady income."

Dave took a job at the Chesapeake Biological Laboratory in Oxford. He worked under the auspices of the U. S. Fish and Wildlife Service. At the lab, Dave worked with the shellfish culture program. "The program experimented with oyster larva," said Dave. "We grew oysters in a variety of ways. We tried growing them on strings like they do in Japan and even went over there to study their methods. Our oyster was a different species than theirs and didn't do well growing on strings.

"We grew oysters in shell bags and on artificial turf. We also experimented with feeding young oysters. We found that they were very picky eaters. After all our attempts, we concluded that the best way to grow young oysters was in conjunction with a seed operation. The state would buy discarded oyster shells from processing plants and plant (place) them in various locations around the Bay where we knew there was a high concentration of oyster larvae. The larvae would eventually attach themselves to the oyster shells and grow to market size. The program was highly successful. From 1962 until the late 1970s, more oysters were produced in the Bay through the seed program than were caught. Unfortunately no statistics were kept to illustrate the effectiveness of the program and funding dried up.

"The state was also leery of spending funds to replenish oyster bars because of the diseases that strike oysters; Dermo and MSX. In the 1980s, a series of droughts raised the salinity of the water. When salinity gets to be over fifteen parts per thousand (ppt) these diseases become active. Below 15 ppt, diseases tend to be dormant. The state was reluctant to sink a lot of money into the program if, in the end, the oysters were ultimately going to die.

"Along with planting oyster shells, the state is currently beginning to experiment with a form of planting using calcified stone rather than discarded oyster shells. Only time will tell if this technique is a success."

Dave was employed at the Oxford Lab until 1977. "By then, NOAA (National Oceanic and Atmospheric Association) had taken over the lab and they were planning to transfer all the ongoing research we were doing to Woods Hole in Massachusetts," Dave said. "I decided to remain close to home rather than moving up north. My dad had become ill by that time also and I started working in the boat shop full time. In 1979, my dad passed away and I took over the operation of the shop."

Dave McQuay's boat shop is nestled along the banks of Jackson's Cove, a tributary of Harris Creek. The shop is a throwback to earlier days when many similar operations were active along the Chesapeake shoreline. Railroad tracks stretch the length of the floor in the 50 by 30-foot building. Lines of fluorescent lights are neatly arranged overhead. Sawdust surrounds a row of power tools along one side of the building. A workbench lines most of the wall space on the same side of the shop. On it is an array of hand tools, neatly stacked and standing at the ready for their next task. On the opposite wall are a series of clamps awaiting utilization. A disconnected furnace stands in one corner of the room and, at the other end, the rails disappear under a wide doorway.

Outside, a 25-foot rectangular cradle rests atop the rails that eventually disappear under the waters of the creek. Boats rest on the cradle as they are being pulled out of the water. The cradle rolls over the tracks on railroad wheels. The railroad tracks stretch for ninety feet and end under six feet of water. When a boat is to be pulled up on the railway, it is floated onto the cradle, positioned, and blocked. The cradle is then pulled forward and the boat is lifted from the water following the path of the rails. Once near the building, McQuay attaches a line with a series of pulleys and the boat enters the building.

"See that one horsepower electric motor over there?" McQuay said as he pointed to the corner of the shop nearest the water. "That is what powers the whole operation. That motor is sitting in the same spot it was when we bought the shop. It was bought at Sears and Roebuck. Neither the motor nor the cable spool has ever been replaced and they've never needed repair. The only maintenance they get is when I blow off the sawdust once in a while.

Cradle awaiting a boat at McQuay's shop.

"The belt is stretched over the motor pulley and then down over a larger wheel attached to a 1969 International truck three speed transmission. A short shaft with a two-inch gear extends from the back of the transmission and is coupled to a 16-inch ring gear which drives the cable."

Amazingly, that little motor enables McQuay to haul boats as long as forty-five feet and weighing as much as twelve tons.

"The track that the boat rides on has to be clean and the wheels on the cradle well lubricated," Dave explained. "If anything gets on the track, the cradle will stop. Barnacles or anything will stop it." Periodically Dave hires a diver to scrape the rails that are underwater. "One time there was a half bushel of oysters attached to the rails," he laughed. "I had enough for a good oyster dinner that night."

The tracks ultimately erode and rust in the area where the tides rise and fall around them. Erosion necessitated the replacement of the rails only once, in 1989. Dave found replacement rails in Reading, Pennsylvania.

A variety of boats have slid down the rails from Dave's shop. "We've built a couple of boats that were eventually used as tour boats in New Jersey," said Dave. "These boats had to meet rigid Coast Guard requirements and pass a stringent inspection process." Additionally, about seventy power boats have been built in the shop. Most of these were made of wood; however, four were manufactured from C-Flex, a fiberglass planking material. Two of these boats were forty-footers and two were twenty-four feet in length. He has also produced about twenty-five row skiffs and a couple of 22-foot sailboats. About twenty gunning skiffs were built by the McQuay's. These were open boats, about 20 feet long with racks built in to store guns and decoys. "We even built a pontoon boat for Senator and Presidential hopeful, Barry Goldwater," Dave stated. "We also built a Japanese bathtub for a retired minister. The tub was chest high and made of wood."

A critical part of the boat-building and repair process, Dave believes, lies in the selection of materials. "The selection of materials for building boats from wood is the key to successful boat-building," said Dave. "We can't use kiln dried lumber. We must search out wood that is suitable for boat building. The keel, for example, must have been cut in winter when the sap isn't running. It must be cut from either side of the heart of the log. Keels can't be cut from the heart because the heart log will split, check, and crack. The first two cuts of lumber off the center of the heart is the best boat lumber.

"The keel is the most important part of the boat. Everything works off the keel. All the stations, bulkheads, transom, cabin, and engine mounts are attached to the keel. Because of this, the keel has to be perfectly level. If it isn't, the boat won't come out right.

"Planking requires lumber with a vertical grain, or quarter grain, rather than side grain. The search for material is time consuming. After we find the proper lumber, we have to let it sit for six months to cure before we can use it.

"It takes years to learn the complete boat building trade. It is a profession that could never be learned without the help of an experienced builder. It's a trade that can't be learned on your own.

"When a customer comes in and wants a boat built in a hurry we can't do it. It takes a while to build out of wood. That's one reason boat building has gone to fiberglass. It's quicker and you don't have to worry about seams. Seams in a wooden boat are problems. They are usually located where stressful joints are and may have a tendency to open and leak.

"Wood boats have advantages, however. They float in the water better than a fiberglass boat. They are also more stable to work from and ride over the waves with an easier motion. They also smell better than fiberglass boats and are easier to repair.

A boat atop a cradle at the entry to the shop.

"Chesapeake watermen were some of the last to go to fiberglass boats. Now, many work from glass boats and even aluminum. Aluminum boats are susceptible to electrolysis. Watermen who own these must take precautions to ward against that.

"Watermen today aren't like their forefathers. Years ago the waterman could put a small engine in his boat and go a short distance and fill his boat with oysters, crabs, and other product. With the ever decreasing supply of seafood, watermen have to travel greater distances to seek out their catch. This necessitates larger boats with more powerful engines. They can't go to a nearby creek like they did years ago to make a livelihood."

In addition to constructing boats, Dave has also restored two skipjacks and four log canoes. He maintains the canoe named *Flying Cloud*. At thirty-five feet, the *Flying Cloud* is one of the largest canoes that sail in the Chesapeake Bay Log Canoe Racing Association. "Johnson Grimes had her built in 1931," said Dave. "He owned the Tidewater Inn in Easton. The *Flying Cloud* first raced in 1932. Because she was six inches too long and had a wine glass stern, racing officials wouldn't allow her to sail for the prestigious Governor's Cup. The Governor's Cup series is held annually at the Miles River Yacht Club in St. Michaels. She was later shortened by six inches and her stern was modified to meet the racing rules."

From 1981 until 1989, Dave skippered the canoe during racing season on the rivers of the Bay. "We won several races during that time," he said. "We won a series trophy in Cambridge and had many second and third place finishes. Many times we finished first but other boats beat us because of the handicapping system assigned to each boat."

Dave McQuay at helm of Flying Cloud.
Courtesy of Dave McQuay.

In addition to his boat business, Dave is the caretaker of an offshore island. "I go over to Coaches Island a couple of times a week to check on things," said Dave. "I do some bush hogging and make sure everything is okay.

"The owners were originally from Jew Jersey but now they mainly split their time between Nantucket and Florida. They bought the 50-acre island in 1982 for use as a place to hunt and fish. They usually visit there in the fall and hunt until about Christmas. Sometimes I'll go over there during hunting season and act as a guide for hunting parties.

"There are a couple of ponds over there and a house trailer was brought over. A forty-foot container is used as a shop and storage. There is also a building that houses the generator."

Dave enjoys hunting and it is his favorite leisure activity. "I love to hunt ducks and geese in the winter," he said. "A group of us have an offshore blind on Tilghman Island and I spend a lot of time there during hunting season."

Dave is also active in community affairs. He is a fifty-year veteran of the Tilghman Fire Department and is a Past President of both the Tilghman Department and the Eastern Shore Fireman's Association. In honor of his service and dedication, he was inducted into the Eastern Shore Fireman's Association Hall of Fame as well as the Maryland State Fireman's Hall of Fame.

A Master Mason, he is very active in Granite Lodge 177 in St. Michaels. He has been a member since 1971 and was the Grand Master in 1977, a position he has again held for the last four years. His father was Master of the same Lodge in 1950.

Twice married, Dave is the father of three. "My first marriage ended in divorce," he said. "I gained custody of my daughter and raised her. Her name is Vicky and she's now forty-five years old. I married my second wife (Helen) in 1977. She is a microbiologist at the Memorial Hospital in Easton. We have two children; a daughter, Jessica, aged 31 and a son, David, who is 28."

Mathematician, architect, businessman, and master of many trades, Dave McQuay continues a tradition that is deeply rooted in his family. Extremely knowledgeable and talented, he has earned wide-spread respect for the skillful manner in which he carries out his craft.

CHAPTER TWO

Stanley Larrimore

"It used to be that in about October, after the first frost, the water would clear up," said Stanley Larrimore. "You could stand on the bow (front) of your boat and watch crabs crawling on the bottom, the water was that clear. There was grass everywhere. In the old days, the grass was so thick that watermen had to use weedless wheels (propellers) on their boats. These were two-bladed wheels rather than three. A three-bladed wheel would get hung up in the grass. There was grass everywhere.

"When I was growing up I was always fooling around the water. We'd have little skiffs and we'd paddle around the cove. We'd make sails for them in the summer and when winter came we'd make ice boats to sail across the ice. I always enjoyed being near the water."

The 83-year-old Larrimore lives in the same house where he was born. "Dr. Reeser brought me into the world," he stated. "He'd bring his wife with him to help with the birth. I was born in that room right over there. They say that when I was born there was a terrible thunder storm going on. It was July 1, 1930."

Stanley's family lived in the settlement of Fairbank, on Tilghman Island. Located on the extreme southern tip of the island, the town borders the waters of Black Walnut Cove. Glendy, Stanley's father, owned and operated a dredge boat during oyster season (October through March).

"Dad kept his dredge boat anchored in the cove and he'd row out to it each day to go to work," Larrimore said. "He'd set two anchors because if the wind hauled around to the northwest the boat might drag and run aground. When the cove would freeze, the whole crew would get into a skiff and stand near the bow. Their weight would force the stern of the skiff out of the water and they'd push the back of the boat up on top of the ice, and then they'd walk back toward the stern and their weight would break the ice. That was hard work. It would take an hour or more just to push through the ice to get aboard the dredge boat.

"Skipjacks and bugeyes used canvas sails in those days. When it was icy, the sails would freeze. The material they were made from would absorb the moisture and ice would form. When ice was on them, you had to raise just a little bit of sail and let the sun melt the ice, then raise a little more and let it melt until you had it all the way up. If you put the sail up all the way at once, the sail would rip because of the weight. Sails in use today aren't like that; they're made from better material."

Stanley's dad owned three dredge boats during his lifetime. His first boat was a bugeye named *Fannie Harrington*. "I don't remember much about the *Harrington*," Stanley said. "She had a square foresail. When her working days were over, she was put up in a marsh right here in this cove, where she wasted away. It was during the Depression and people couldn't make a living. Oysters weren't bringing much money and it was hard to survive. There were two other boats laid up over in the cove. Later on the state came and removed one of the boats, a bugeye named the *H. M. Dougherty*."

The elder Larrimore's last boat was a skipjack named *Laura J. Evans*. "There are boats that are smart and there's boats that are dumb," Stanley smiled. "The *Evans* was one of the dumb ones. She'd sail real good in heavy air, but, in light air, when she came about, she'd come up into the wind and that's where she'd stop. She wouldn't go any farther; she'd just lay there and flap her sails. Dad would get mad, stomp his feet, and complain. He did everything to try to change her. He tried to extend her rudder by attaching long pieces of rubber on either side, but that didn't make any difference. Dad always compared her to his second skipjack, *Laura M. Barclay*.

"Now if the *Evans* was a dumb boat, the *Barclay* was a smart one. She sailed really well. She was just as quick as could be. She had a plug rudder (rudder was inside the boat) whereas the *Evans* had an outside rudder (hung from the stern). She was a small skipjack. She could only carry about 150 bushels or so. She had a small cabin up forward. She ended up in Deal Island. I don't know where the *Evans* ended up.

"Dad had a little trouble with another dredger one time. He and another boat were in close proximity to each other. When the other boat went by one of dad's crew members heard the captain say something about how dad had cut him off. He said that he was going to run over dad. He came about (changed direction) and headed for dad. Neither boat would give way and both held their course. He came by, ran into dad and broke his bow sprit (the pole like extension protruding from the bow of the boat on which the jib sail is attached).

"Dad also turned the *Barclay* over one time. They were dredging and Dad saw what he thought was rain on the horizon headed for them. He called the cook down in the cabin to hand him his oilskins in preparation for the rain. It turned out that it wasn't rain at all, it was wind. When the gust of wind hit the boat, she turned over. One of the crew members walked up over the boat as she rolled over and didn't even get his feet wet. After she finished rolling over, he asked the other crew members in the water if any of them had a match."

In 1947, Stanley began working on the *Laura M. Barclay* with his father. "I had finished the tenth grade in school, but didn't go back for my final year," he said. "My father pleaded with me to go back and finish, but I wanted to be out there on the water. After I started working with him, he gave me the dirtiest and worst jobs on the boat. Even with that, I still didn't want to go back to school. We had some lean years about that time. We didn't make much money. Most days we'd only catch eighteen bushels or so."

A few years later, oysters were once again plentiful. "We were dredging near Sharp's Island one day," Stanley continued. "We sailed up right close to the island and it was loaded with oysters. We caught 329 bushels of oysters that day. We had a jag on board. There were no catch limits in those days. They were great big oysters and we got $2 a bushel for them. The next day, it seemed like every dredger in the Bay came to Sharp's Island to work."

After dredging season was over in early spring, Stanley worked as a crewmember with a pound netter. He was 16 when he started. Pound nets were set in the spring of the year. "We'd start skinning pine poles in March," said Larrimore. "These would be driven down into the bottom and the net would be attached to them in about thirty feet of water. As the fish swam by, they would strike the net and follow it to a rounded crib, or heart, where they would stay. We'd go out and dip the fish out of the crib. Sometimes we'd catch ten or twelve tons of fish in a day. We'd start at three or four in the morning and wouldn't get home until sundown. I made $60 a week when I started. One day the owner of the net came to me and told me he was going to raise me up to $100 a week because I was doing as much work as any of the men in the crew. That was a lot of money in those days. We'd fish all summer until it was time to go back dredging.

"One morning, we were headed down the Bay for a place called The Gooses. We had a net down there and we saw bright lights coming from that direction. The owner of the boat was puzzled by the lights because, ordinarily, there weren't any lights in that vicinity. He checked the compass to make sure he was headed in the right direction and everything checked out. As we got closer to Sharp's Island we saw a PT boat all lit up. The boat had run aground on the southern tip of the island. She was two hundred feet or more up on the island. That was right after the war, in 1946 or '47. They got her off pretty quick; she wasn't there very long."

Chesapeake weather has always been a concern for the watermen of the Bay. "During the storm of 1933 they told me that the *Barclay* broke loose from her mooring and came ashore," Stanley explained. "She landed in a farmer's field, a long distance from the water. Cows were all around her. Captain John B. Harrison built a skid for her and they put rollers under it and got that boat right back overboard where she had been before the storm. That must have been quite a job. Those boys knew what they were doing in those days."

Married on his birthday in 1950, Stanley received a draft notice in October of the same year. "I went up to Baltimore to take my physical and found out that I was being drafted into the Marine Corps," he said. "I went to Cambridge when I got home and signed up for the Navy. The Korean War was going on at that time. I stayed in the Navy for 4-1/2 years." Returning home in 1956, after his discharge from the Navy, Stanley crabbed in the summers using crab pots.

Crab pots, made from wire, often referred to as chicken wire, are approximately two feet square with openings near the bottom on each of the four sides. Bait, usually menhaden, is placed in the center of the pot in a funnel. Crabs enter the pot through the openings in pursuit of the bait. Realizing they are caught, their natural inclination is to swim upward through one of two openings in the interior of the pot. The crab remains at this point until the crabber removes it from its watery captivity.

"Right after the war I crab-potted with my brother," said Stanley. "We only had one hundred pots in those days; that's all we were allowed. We hauled our crabs to Kent Island every day. There was a better market up there. We crabbed in a boat named *Elsie B*. She's laid up now on the shore down by the Narrows." Later, Stanley trot-lined for crabs.

"I also drove a crab truck to New York four nights a week," continued Stanley. "I'd leave home at three or four in the afternoon bound for New York. I'd go crabbing in the mornings before I left for New York. I'd start crabbing at 4 a.m. They gave me $100 a week to drive the truck."

Stanley crabbed during the summers until two years ago. "I was crab potting again by that time," he explained. "My wife, Loretta, went with me every day. She'd steer the boat and I'd pull the pots and cull (sort) the crabs. Once in a while she'd miss a pot and I'd say something to her. She'd get mad and tell me she was going to quit on me. I told her there wouldn't be any need to quit because I had no intention of taking her in to shore — she'd still have to stay out there, so she might as well steer the boat. Loretta would meet me on shore and bring me breakfast just before we went crabbing. I'd pick her up and she'd stay on the boat with me after that. I enjoyed that more than any other time that I crabbed."

Following his stint in the Navy, Stanley bought half interest in a skipjack named *Reliance*. The owner found himself in financial difficulty and sold a portion to Stanley. The *Reliance* was forty-one feet on deck with a fourteen-foot beam (width). She was built in the town of Oriole in Somerset County in 1904. Stanley dredged her for a few years and shared the earnings with his partner. "It seemed like I was doing all the work and my partner was getting all the money," laughed Larrimore. "I told him that there had to be some changes. Either I had to sell out my share or he had to sell out his share. It turned out that I bought his share and things were a lot better after that.

"One year I had her on the railway. It was September and almost time for dredging season. I had noticed a soft spot near a chainplate. I started taking out rotten wood; the rot went up to the bow to the stem and around to the stern and one-third the way up the other side. I replaced all that wood. I stopped there and went dredging. I didn't realize she was that bad; she was rotten all over. After dredging season, I finished replacing the rest of the rotted wood."

Stanley sold the *Reliance* to a college student from southern Maryland. The boat was dredged for only one more year. The owner had placed a sump pump in the boat and electrolysis ate through all the fasteners. When the boat was eventually hauled on the railway, the bottom fell out. Stanley related that she was hauled at the Dennis Pont Marina and, after the boat was discarded, the marina used her mast for a flagpole.

In January 1975, Stanley bought the skipjack *Lady Katie*. She was built in 1956 by the legendary boat-builder Bronza Parks in Wingate, south of Cambridge; Parks had a reputation as an excellent craftsman. The boat had pleasant lines and was pleasing to the eye. *Lady Katie* was forty-six feet on deck with a seventeen-and-a-half-foot beam. "She was really a nice boat," said Stanley. "She was a smart boat, she was the best dredge boat I ever put my foot on. I really loved that boat."

Stanley dredged for oysters in *Lady Katie* during the season. "I took six crew members with me when I dredged," Stanley said. "When we were on the oyster bar three men were stationed on each side of the boat, two forward and one aft. Their job was to work the dredges. Dredges were lifted out of the water by a donkey engine on the deck of the boat. In the old days they were winched aboard by hand. That was a rough job. A loaded dredge might weigh close to 1,000 pounds. There was a dredge set from both sides of the boat, that's why the men worked in teams. The men also helped with sail handling. Sometimes several men were needed to tend the sails when a good breeze was blowing."

The triangular dredges were of different design. "I carried ten dredges with me," said Stanley. "There were five pairs on either side; which pair we used depended on what the bottom was like. We had dredges that were used on muddy bottoms. Edge dredges were used on slightly harder bottoms. Hard dredges and flat plate dredges were used on even harder bottoms. On rock, gum dredges were used. You had to know what the bottom was like. In the days before electronic navigation, we used long poles to sound

The skipjack *Lady Katie* under sail.
Courtesy of Stanley Larrimore.

along the bottom. We'd use it to sound over the bottom and when it came up on some oysters you could feel them as the pole dragged through them."

One day, Stanley was dredging in dense fog. "It was thick foggy," he said. "When the dredge line came taught, the boat stopped. The dredge was hung up on something. We tried everything we knew, but we couldn't get the dredge back aboard. I finally cut the line and threw out a marker so I'd know where the dredge was located. Later, on a dish ca'am (very calm) day, my brother and I went back to try and get the dredge. We threw anchors out and snagged it and tried to bring it aboard, but we couldn't bring it up. Finally, we just gave up and left it there. My guess is that it was dropped over top of a rock and got hung up down there."

Like many watermen who depend on their crew, Stanley had difficulties from time to time. "I was having a little trouble with the crew one year," he said. "I told them if they hadn't got themselves straight by the following Friday I was going to go to Florida

Culling oysters aboard the *Lady Katie*.
Courtesy of Stanley Larrimore.

and they wouldn't earn any wages. 'No, you won't do that,' one of the crew members told me. A freeze up came a few days later and I packed up and went to Florida until the thaw came. I had so much trouble with the crew another time that I went dredging all by myself. It wasn't easy doing all that work by myself. I really had a job getting the yawl boat back aboard. I caught twelve or fifteen bushels that day."

In the summer, Stanley began a charter service in the *Lady Katie*. "I was probably the first to do that in a skipjack," he said. "Now, a lot of skipjacks take people out for charters. I took passengers out for twelve years. We'd go for two or three days at a time. Sometimes we'd stay out for a week or so. I built a cabin up forward; we called it the honeymoon suite. There were three bunks there and a head (restroom). On one side of the centerboard well, I built another cabin and even put carpeting in there. On the other side of the centerboard well was another head. A lot of the people preferred to sleep on deck. There was an awning that covered the deck and kept off the morning dew."

Stanley had earned a U. S. Coast Guard license to take passengers. The boat, however, was limited to carrying six passengers because it was not certified by the Coast Guard. The certification process involved a rigid inspection by Coast Guard personnel.

"I had the boat hauled up on the railway over to Mayo one year and decided to have her inspected by the Coast Guard," Stanley said. "The inspector came there and pulled out his tools and started putting on his overalls. He looked at the boat and said, 'I'll tell you one thing right now before we get started, all that cooper sheathing on the sides of the boat will have to be pulled off so I can see what's under it.' (Dredge boats had cooper plating nailed along their waterlines in order to prevent damage to the hull while cutting through ice.) I tried to reason with him and suggested that he take a piece off here and there for the inspection. He disagreed and said all of it would need to be removed. I told him, 'Let me tell you one thing, you can get right back into your truck and head back to Baltimore because I'm not taking that cooper off.' He took off his overalls, got back in his truck, and that was the last, and only, time I ever tried to have her inspected."

Stanley sailed around the rivers and anchored in creeks overnight. Loretta would prepare the food in advance for the charter. "It was real nice, I enjoyed every minute of it," Stanley smiled. "One time I had a party on the boat and the man told me to sail anywhere I wanted but be sure it was a place where he could see plenty of geese. I headed up the Choptank River and anchored in Trappe Creek. It was fall and the next morning it was so foggy you couldn't see your hand in front of you. But there were geese all around the boat; they were everywhere. Those people sat up all night watching the geese. I fulfilled his wish that time."

Every year a group of female artists would charter the boat for a week. As the boat sailed around the creeks, they would sketch and paint. "They told me they'd like to go down to Deal Island," Stanley explained. "When we got there, we tied to the county wharf. It was really hot that day. There was a crab-picking plant nearby and the women got a whiff of that and wanted to move. I told them they'd have to wait until morning 'cause I wouldn't leave in the night. The next day was even hotter than it had been the day before. There was very little wind and the water was calm. We shoved off for home and got out in the Bay near the Hooper's Island Light. The sun was boiling down on us and, with no wind, it seemed like we were inside an oven. The women decided to go for a swim in order to cool off. Some of them had bathing suits, but some didn't. They all jumped over the side. The ones with no suits jumped into the water wearing only their undergarments. After they had finished swimming, they hung their wet clothing up in the rigging to dry. A tugboat came by, saw the underwear, and blew and blew his horn. I guess we gave them something to talk about that day."

Larrimore took one crewmember with him during those trips. "I took a man with me who was also part of my dredging crew in the winter," he said. "He was a nice guy and we got along well. He and I shared the aft cabin. I'd buy a large bottle of aspirin and keep it aboard the boat in case anyone needed it and I noticed that the bottle seemed like it was always empty. The mate was taking them. I thought he was hung up on them or something and I threatened to not replace them. He went crazy and begged me not to do that.

"We were anchored in the Wye River shortly after that and he got sick and went down in the cabin and that's where he stayed. He wouldn't eat or drink anything. He was in a way. We came home on a Sunday and I sent him up to the Marine Hospital in Baltimore. The following Wednesday I was planning to go up to see him and I got word that he had died.

Loretta Larrimore.
Courtesy of Stanley Larrimore.

"There was a man who had chartered the boat quite a bit who lived in Gettysburg, Pennsylvania. He owned a restaurant up there and he'd often bring down members of his staff and go out with me. His name was George Moose and he had told me that if I ever needed crew, to let him know. I called him and he came down and worked with me for the next five or six years. He even went out with me dredging one time.

"We were dredging in the Choptank River near Howell's Point the day that George was on the boat. We had caught our limit of oysters when I noticed a storm brewing. It was about 11 a.m. and it kept breezing up and breezing up, but I thought I could make it home without any problem. We headed for home. By the time we got to Knapps Narrows, the seas were as high as this ceiling. The seas were so bad that we couldn't put the yawl boat down. We were sailing with just a tiny bit of sail up. In the Narrows, the tide and the wind were going in the same direction and we couldn't slow down enough to put down the yawl boat. We called the bridge tender and told him to open the bridge. He opened and we sailed right on through. There must've been fifty or more people standing on the bank watching us as we sailed through. George asked me what they were doing there. I told him they were there to watch us crack up as we went through the Narrows. When we got through the bridge, we had a chance to come about and headed her into the wind and tide. The shelter of the Narrows allowed us to put down the yawl boat and we got her docked. The storm turned out to be a bad one; it was one of those perfect storms. George never went dredging with me again after that."

Stanley has had his share of mishaps during his years of working the waters of the Bay. "I've broken just about everything on a dredge boat that I could," he laughed. "I've broken a bow sprit, a mast, a rudder, and a centerboard while I was out there dredging."

The bow sprit broke on *Reliance*. "There was a rotten place on it and I didn't know it was there" said Stanley. "I also had to replace the bow sprit on *Lady Katie*. I went down to Snow Hill and bought the lumber to build a new bow sprit. I brought it back and put it in my yard. For two years, I poured kerosene on it to cure it. A fellow dredger came and shaped it for me. That thing was varnished up and it looked as good as a stick of candy. After it was finished, I noticed that small holes about a half inch in circumference would come out of it from time to time. I'd plug up the hole and glue a plug in it. Later, I found out that there were bugs inside there and they were chewing their way out.

"We were dredging over to Stone Rock one day in the *Reliance* and the wind breezed up. I told the men that the next time we go about I'd like to reef the main and jib. Before we could come about, the mast broke. It crashed down over the side of the boat and fell into the water. We were lucky it didn't land on the boat and hurt somebody. We had a mess to deal with. We struggled to get the mast, with all that sail attached, back on the boat. After we finally got it back aboard, we centered the mast across the boat to take it in to shore. It was rough and the seas were high. The boat would dip from side to side in the waves and when she'd dip down in a trough the end of the mast would go into the water. We were afraid the seas were going to knock it off the boat but we made it back.

"I broke the rudder on the *Lady Katie*. We had been planting seed oysters for the state down in the southern part of the Bay when I noticed that I lost steerage. After examining the situation, I found that I only had a little piece of the rudder below the water line. Most of the rudder had fallen off.

"We got a tow into Solomons and went to a marina. The boat wouldn't fit in their travel lift, so they just lifted the stern enough so that it cleared the water. We were able to repair the rudder and left Solomons after supper. When we left Solomons, headed for home, the Bay was calm. There was no wind and the water was as slick as glass. I had called Loretta and asked her to drive down to Deal Island and meet us at 11 p.m. that evening. There was just one man on the boat with me. When we got off Hooper

30

Island Light, the breeze picked up. The wind hit us on the nose and we couldn't make any headway. The boy on the boat with me got seasick. The force of the wind allowed us to barely make progress toward Deal Island. It was a wonder we weren't both drowned that night. We didn't get in until 4 a.m. Loretta was worried about us. She had been there for hours and was driving up and down the shore looking for us. When I finally got home, I walked into a house full of people; it was Easter Sunday. I told them they'd have to excuse me, went upstairs, and went to bed.

"On the *Reliance* we were dredging one day and I guess I had the board down too far. The centerboard on the *Reliance* was twelve feet or more in length. It was rough that day and it broke off as it went across the bottom. The same boat was hit by lightning twice. We had a citizens' band radio aboard and lightning hit the antenna and followed it down the mast to a chain plate. It went out the side of the boat and took out a big chunk of wood beside the chain plate."

Despite the many hardships of working on the water, Stanley has enjoyed several unique experiences. In July of 1984, *Lady Katie* was visited by President Ronald Reagan. "During his administration, there was a movement to clean up the Chesapeake Bay," said Stanley. "A fellow who was living on the island arranged for the President's visit to Tilghman. He said there was to be a press conference with Reagan aboard the *Lady Katie*. The morning of Reagan's visit, the Secret Service came and divers examined every boat that was in the harbor. There was security everywhere. Snipers were in the trees and in the marshes around where the boat was moored. They told me to raise the sails on my boat to shield the President, and then they brought in a crab truck and put it on the other side. The secret service examined the crab truck and found that it had a load of crabs inside. They said they'd have to go through every bushel of crabs in that truck for security reasons. They opened the first basket and those crabs waved and snapped their claws at them in an angry manner. They just looked at the crabs and said that they looked like good old American crabs to them. They didn't examine any more crabs after that.

"Reagan's helicopter landed in the schoolyard and his limousine brought him over to Dogwood harbor where our skipjacks were moored. He got on my boat and the reporters asked him lots of questions and took pictures. When it was over, we all went over to the fire hall for lunch. We were told to ride in his limousine. As I got into the limousine, a couple of local guys were already in the back seat so I sat between them. When Reagan approached the car he told me I was in his seat so I had to move to the front and sit next to James Baker, Reagan's Chief of Staff. Reagan made a joke about the situation and he was pleasant to get along with. When they shut the door on that limousine, it sounded like we were in a vault. I did notice that during our ride to the firehouse he kept waving along the way. There was no one there to wave to; he seemed to have lost it, I thought. Right after that, they said he had Alzheimer's."

The *Lady Katie* was also used in two commercials. The first was for a bank. "There were two skipjacks used in the commercial," Stanley explained. "Cameramen were on both boats and one time, as the boats sailed by each other, the boats were so close that the camera was knocked overboard. We didn't get any money for that commercial, but we did for the next one.

"The second one was for a beer company. In that commercial, five skipjacks came into port in the evening, supposedly following a day's work on the Bay. The idea was that after we had landed, we went and had a beer. It took a week or more to make the commercial. It was shown a lot on TV. It even aired during the Super Bowl. They paid us $500 a day. We told them that's how much we could have made if we'd come in with a full jag of oysters, so that's what they paid us.

LADY KATIE

"I took my son, Steve, with me on the boat during the making of the beer commercial. He had real long hair in those days and he even went and got a haircut when he found out he was going to be in the commercial. He didn't want to get a haircut, but he thought it was worth it to be on TV. As it turned out, they didn't use the part he was in; he wasn't too happy about that.

"Steve works over to Oxford in a boat yard over there. He still crabs on weekends and his days off during the season. He was with me in 1977 when the Bay froze up bad. I told him then that he'd better find a better job than working on the water. My daughter, Rhonda, lives over in Delaware. She's a year younger than Steve."

In 1989, Stanley sold his beloved *Lady Katie* and retired from dredging. "I sold her because I could see that she needed about $10,000 worth of work," said Stanley. "I was also getting older and didn't feel like rebuilding her."

Since his retirement from dredging, Stanley and Loretta spend their winters in Florida. "We like it down there, it's a good change of scenery," he said. "We've been going down there for the last fifteen or twenty years. We've gotten to know people from all over the country and we've made lots of good friends. We look forward to seeing them each year. When we go down there, it's like going home.

"I told someone that if I had one wish before I died, I'd wish for the Bay to dry up for a day or so. I'd just like to see what's out there on the bottom. I think it would be fascinating. It would be amazing to see all the things that are on the bottom.

"Of all the things I've done on the water, dredging was my most enjoyable activity. I remember that I couldn't sleep the night before dredging season started, I'd be so excited. I couldn't wait to go dredging, I loved it that much. I liked the sailing part of it. It's an art to get the boat sailing at just the right speed and on the right track for dredging. When it's done right, there's a great feeling of accomplishment. I'm satisfied with the life I've had.

"I wouldn't take anything for my experiences on the water. I've had my ups and my downs, but I have a lot of respect for the Chesapeake. I also have a lot of respect for those that work on the Bay. They have to know many things. It doesn't matter how much or how little education they have, they are pretty smart when it comes to dealing with the many situations they are faced with."

Epilogue: Loretta Larrimore died during the summer of 2012. Loretta was a charming lady who was a constant support for her husband. Her warm smile will be missed.

President Reagan signing the log book aboard the *Lady Katie*;
George Moose is in the white shirt. *Courtesy of Stanley Larrimore.*

CHAPTER THREE

Chris Skinner

"When other boys in the neighborhood were playing baseball and football, I was down on the riverbank," said Chris Skinner. "Our house was right on the river and I spent a lot of my time down there. The other kids called me a river rat. I just loved fooling around the river. There were five of us kids in our family and nobody gave us anything. If we wanted something, we had to go out and get the money to buy it. If I wanted a bike, I'd go down to the river and catch fish or muskrats and save up my money till I could pay for it." Of the five children in the family, Chris was the youngest. There were three older brothers and a sister. Their father commuted daily to Wilmington, Delaware, where he worked in an automobile manufacturing plant.

Along with his brother, Chris' dad was a part-time fisherman. They fished only to catch enough to feed their sizeable family. The family lived among the picturesque rolling hills that border the upper reaches of the Chester River. Located on the riverbank, their house was part of the small town of Crumpton, about fifteen miles from Chestertown. "I spent my youth in that house in Crumpton," said Chris. "I loved living there; it was a Tom Sawyer existence. When dad sold it later on, I was really devastated.

"When I was ten or eleven years old, I'd go around and set nets for fish. You didn't need a license back then; all you had to do was put your name on a stake and nail that to your net. I set a net in front of our house and rowed out to it in a skiff. My net was all ripped up and not in the best of shape, but I caught as many or more fish than some of the commercial guys further down the river. I'd catch more fish than we could eat and would go around the neighborhood giving them away. My neighbors loved me for that. In season, I'd give them muskrats, geese, and ducks also. Whatever they wanted, I'd get for them. There aren't many of those old folks left around here now. Most of the people that live here now have (recently) moved in.

"A few years later, my uncle died and I bought his fishing boat. It was made of plywood, sixteen feet long, and it had a 4-horsepower outboard motor on the stern.

34

With that boat, I was able to venture further away to fish and hunt. One day, the marine police came along and confiscated my net. By then, the state had started issuing licenses to fish, crab, and hunt. After my net was taken away, my dad told me, 'Come on and go with me. We're going down to Centreville and get you a commercial license.' I'll never forget it; that license cost $12.50. I was about fourteen or fifteen at the time."

One day in early February, when Chris was a teenager, he told his father that he was going to set a drift net out in the river and see what he could catch. Drift nets are about fifty yards in length and have weights along their bottom edge. Along the top of the net are floats that allow the net to float on the surface. The fish that swim by are caught as they attempt to get through the webbing of the net.

"Dad told me I was crazy, no fish come up the river 'til March," explained Chris. "I told him I was going to try it anyway. It was an unseasonably warm day and I laid out my net and came back to the house, planning to fish the net the next morning. The next day, I woke up and there was a foot of snow on the ground and it was bitter cold. By the time I got out of the house, another foot of snow had fallen. It was snowing so hard that you couldn't see where you were going. The snowflakes actually hurt when they hit your face. The river was starting to slush up; I had to go out and retrieve my net. My brother was with me and when we got to the net, it was full of white perch. White perch were wall-to-wall. We started pulling the net in and it began to freeze against the side of the boat. After a long struggle, we finally got the net aboard and headed toward shore. The motor was running wide open and we were barely making headway through the ice.

"When we got on shore, we tried to get the net out of the boat. The fish were frozen to the boat's bottom. We went to the house and got a shovel to free them from the boat. The fish were all tangled up in the net and it was rolled up in a big ball. My father came down and asked how we were going to get the fish out. I told him we were going to take the net, with the fish, down to the basement in front of the wood stove and thaw them out. That's exactly what we did. As each fish came out of the net, we just put them outside in a basket. That way they were naturally refrigerated. We ended up getting three or four feet of snow during that storm."

Chris attended schools in the nearby town of Sudlersville for his elementary and middle school years. For high school, he attended Queen Anne High in Centreville, graduating in 1985. A few years later, Chris got married. "My wife, Susan, raises Newfoundland dogs," Chris explained. "These are big dogs. Our male goes 165 pounds and the female 145. They are gentle giants. They wouldn't hurt anybody. They may lick you to death though. Susan also does obedience training for other people. We have two kids, a boy who is 21 and a girl, 20. We even have a grandbaby, a boy. Susan also has a commercial crabbing license. She often goes with me in the summers. She's a big help."

Chris uses fike nets for fishing these days. Fike nets are circular in design and are set close to shore. A lead, or hedging, is set near the bank. Fish bump into the lead on their way up and down stream and follow it into deeper water. At the end of the lead is the trap where the fish gather until they are harvested.

Chris was inserting poles into the river bottom in anticipation of setting a fike net one day. "It was very cold," he said. "There was eighteen feet of water where I was working. To get the poles to sink into the river bottom, I would stand on the gunnels of the boat and push them down using all my body weight. I'd do this over and over until the pole got down to the depth I wanted it. I was working on the last piling and I pushed the pole down and it struck a rock or something on the bottom and didn't go in. Instead, it bounced off the bottom and threw me away from my boat. I was hanging onto that pole while the boat floated away. The pole was bending and I ended up in the cold water. I didn't know what to do. Should I let go and swim toward the boat or swim toward the shore. I decided to head for the boat. I had on waders (a protective rubber suit that stretches from the feet to the armpit) and when I got to the boat I couldn't get in because my waders were full of water. Finally, I had enough sense to go around to the back of the boat and use the lower unit of the motor to step up into the boat. I dumped what felt like two hundred gallons of water out of my waders after getting into the boat. It's funny now, but when it happened it wasn't so funny.

"I used to set up to six fike nets, but now I only set three. Fishing's gone bad. The state stopped me from fishing up here (headwaters of the Chester). They say that this is where the fish come to spawn. I haven't been able to fish this far up the river for five years and the fish haven't rebounded. There aren't as many now as there were before they made us stop fishing up here. Overfishing is not the problem; I think pollution is the main culprit.

"They put in a new sewage treatment plant up in Millington, at the head of the river, and it's located in a flood plain. I've seen it overflow twice. And you know where the stuff ends up-right in the Chester River. It's a shame, really.

"Another factor is construction. Everybody who builds a house on the waterfront puts in a pier, it seems. Many times that pier might be blocking an inshore channel that fish follow on their way upstream. I can show you three or four piers right in this area that are located like that. After this happens, fish won't go up the river any more. It has a devastating effect on fishing.

"The DNR (Department of Natural Resources) places catch limits on each river. In the Chester River, only 6,000 pounds of yellow perch are allowed to be caught each year. That's fine for the boys who fish down by the mouth of the river, but by the time the fish migrate up to the headwaters where I fish, most of the quota has already been caught. I'm one of the last men on the totem pole. What they should do is set up a quota for each commercial fisherman so it would be fair. It's so bad that I don't even fish for yellow perch anymore.

"It takes a lifetime to learn where to set nets to catch fish. You can set a net in one place and catch plenty of fish. If you set another one 150 feet away from the first, you might not catch a thing. The water depth and the bottom type are two of the many factors you need to know when you go fishing. A good day now, with three fikes, might yield one hundred pounds of fish. At 25 cents a pound, that isn't much of a reward. By the time you consider gasoline for my truck and boat, the cost of the nets, licenses, and other factors, I don't take home a whole lot of money at the end of the day.

"In the old days, we'd sell fish right from the house in Crumpton. Some days we'd sell 1,000 pounds of fish. Wednesday was an especially good day for selling. Hundreds of people would come to Crumpton to go to the auction. That was just up the road from us. Word got around that we sold fish and a lot of those people would stop by. We usually sold all we had in no time. Some of those people still buy from me even though I no longer live in Crumpton. I've had some customers for twenty-five or thirty years. These people also buy muskrats from me in season.

"I used to paint houses until crabbing season started. I'd fish and trap part-time on days after I finished painting. The economy took care of that. What little building is going on now is being done by crews from the western shore. They bring their own paint crews with them. I've only painted about a week in the past year."

In 1990, the state placed a moratorium on rockfish (striped bass) fishing. Officials felt that some time was needed to replenish the stock. "I was fishing for perch one day right after the rockfish moratorium went into effect," said Chris. "Instead of perch, big rockfish got into my nets. When I pulled up my nets, there were ninety-one rockfish in them. They were all dead because the nets were too small for them. I put them in my boat; each one weighed between twenty and twenty-five pounds. I wasn't sure what to do with the fish. A friend of mine suggested that I sell them to a buyer that he knew. The buyer turned out to be an undercover cop. I was arrested and told that I could get up to a year of jail time and a $500 fine for each fish I had caught — that would've been ninety-one years. Plus, they could take my license and confiscate my boat, truck, nets, and anything else I had. Jeezoo! I was sweating that one. I went to court and was fined $500 and given ninety days in jail. The judge put me on work release. My case was on TV and in the newspaper. I was a dirty so and so for that one. I've never done anything like that again. When I catch an oversize fish now, I throw it back right away.

"One day I had just pulled in my net and a big rockfish was tangled in it. A DNR guy pulled up beside me just as I took the fish out of the net. I told him that the fish was not very healthy. It was on its last legs. I suggested that he take the fish to a nursing home or someplace where it could be eaten. He said no and told me to throw it overboard. That fish didn't get any more than a boat length away before it turned belly up and died. What a shame that was. I really felt bad because it was such a waste."

Chris is very concerned about wildlife. When an animal that has the potential to feed a family dies without its ultimate use as a food source, it affects him negatively. "I hate to see anything go to waste," he said. "It just tears me up to know that there are people out there without food on their tables who could've made use of that animal."

In addition to other challenges, Chris must also deal with intruders. "It used to be when I fished up by the bridge, there were great blue herons and eagles that would wait for me just about every day," Chris laughed. "When I'd pull in the nets, the birds would fight to see who could steal a fish. There was a culling board on top of my boat and I'd put all the fish on that until I had a chance to throw the small ones back into the river. Those birds would wait and steal fish as they came off the culling board. One old heron landed right on the bow of my boat and stood there. I threw a small fish toward him and that dude caught it right in midair."

Chris was finishing up fishing for the day and he saw a DNR boat headed toward him with a good turn of speed. The DNR boat was outside the channel and Chris watched as it struck a mud flat at wide open speed. "They were stuck," he chuckled. "They weren't going anywhere. They asked if I could pull them off. I told them I couldn't get close enough to them to throw them a line or I'd be on the bottom myself. I told them they'd be able to get off in a couple of hours when the tide came up."

Chris caught three rainbow trout in his nets while fishing once. "It freaked me out," he said. "I couldn't figure out how those fish got way up here in the river. I found out later that they were released from the wildlife refuge upriver and swam down this way and got into my net. I also caught an albino catfish once. He was snow white and he had pink eyes and everything. There's a picture of the fish right up the road in the store."

Chris Skinner's yearly activities are defined by the seasons. From February until early March he roams the marshes in search of muskrats. Beginning in March, until about April 15th, he sets his fike nets. Following fishing season he sets traps for turtles until crabbing season starts on May 1st. Thereafter, he crabs until November.

During the cold of winter, Chris traps muskrats. Muskrats are marsh-dwelling members of the rodent family, about a foot in length, and weighing about four pounds. They are highly prized for their pelts. Before the days of animal rights, many muskrat pelts were made into fur coats; very desirable for the well-dressed set.

Now, the pelts are sent to far-off countries where they remain a valuable material for clothing. When prepared properly, muskrats are a genuine delicacy, still savored on the Eastern Shore. Muskrats build houses out of short tree branches gathered from the marsh. The houses are easily spotted in the marsh. They are domed structures, about six feet or so in diameter, and about three feet high. The muskrat utilizes an underwater entrance (the lead) to get into its house. To trap the muskrat, a steel trap is pushed up into the lead as far as possible and, as the muskrat enters, the muskrat is caught. The hunter merely pulls out the trap and extracts the muskrat.

"One day, when I was fifteen years old, I was trapping for muskrats," Chris smiled. "Back then, I would catch a couple of hundred in a season. Dad came to me one day and told me he needed a truck to haul firewood but didn't have the money to buy one. I told him I thought I had enough money saved up to buy one. Later, when we took the furs in to the buyer, I handed over enough money for him to buy that truck. That was some truck. It had a three-speed shift on the steering column. We ran that truck for a lot of years after that."

In a good year, Chris sells his muskrats to a local dealer. "Brown pelts bring about $9, black pelts can bring as high as $11," he said. "Of course when the market is bad, the price goes way down. Sometimes we only get $5 or less for a hide."

Through the years, Chris has had his share of mishaps. "One time, when I was about twenty years old, I'd gone out into the marsh and set my traps," he stated. "After they were set, a flood tide came along and water came overtop the marsh. I was carrying about twenty muskrats in my coat and in a sack at the time when I went into the flooded marsh. I knew there was a deep ditch on the way to my traps and when I got to it I tried to jump over it. I forgot about the extra weight of the muskrats I was carrying and fell flat on my face into the icy water in the ditch. I sat up on a muskrat hut and took my hip boots off and emptied them. My boat was about fifty yards away and I headed for it. It was very cold. I almost didn't make it. My legs started to freeze up and wouldn't move like they should. I was in the beginning stages of hypothermia. I finally crawled to my boat on all fours, pushed it off the marsh and somehow was able to start the engine. I was laying right flat in the boat's bottom, I couldn't sit up. I ran that boat right up onto the boat ramp. She was wide open. When I hit the ramp, it tore the bottom off the boat. She was high and dry. I struggled to get to my truck, started it and ran the heater on full blast for about thirty minutes or so. Good Lord a Moses! I almost died that day. It scared the bejeezus out of me!"

This year muskrats have not been plentiful. In fact, Chris thinks this is the worst year he has ever experienced. "I think the weather is to blame," he said. "It's been so mild that the muskrats don't have to leave their houses. They store up food in their houses for the winter. I think they stored enough food in their houses to last and there was no need for them to go outside. They anticipated a hard winter. They won't start moving again until mating season."

Between fishing and crabbing season, Chris traps snapping turtles. Turtle traps are similar to fish traps. They are set along the shoreline and they have four rings in them and a double funnel where the bait is deposited.

"The turtles go in after the bait (chopped shad)," Chris said. "Once they're back in the end of the trap, they are caught. I have to put a float in each trap so the turtles can have something to crawl up on so they can breathe. Turtles have to be 10-1/2" from the front of the shell to the back of the shell to be of legal size. Smaller ones have to be thrown back. There is no catch limit for the number of turtles you catch.

"I sell them to a guy in Millington. They are processed right there and most are sold in this area as delicacies. Lots of local restaurants serve snapper soup. The area

On the dock after a day of crabbing.

around the town of North East serves lots of snapper soup in their restaurants. They really like it up there. Female turtles are sent to China. They're valuable for their eggs over there. I'll set about twenty turtle traps. I use turtling to carry me over till crabbing season starts."

Chris' primary yearly income comes from crabbing. The Chesapeake Bay provides most of the crabs that are consumed in the United States. Like Chris, most of the folks who work the water rely on crabbing as their main source of income.

Skinner uses a method called trotlining to gather his crabs. Chris' trotlines are 2,000 feet in length and he utilizes two of these lines in his daily pursuit of the crab. Trotlines rest on the bottom and, as the crab hangs onto the bait, the line is gently lifted to the surface by the boat's momentum. As the crab nears the surface, the trotliner dips it off the line with a net.

"In the early part of the season, from early May until the water warms to about seventy degrees, we use razor clams for bait," said Chris. "The clams are crushed and placed in small bags, then tied to the trotline. After the water gets warm, we use chicken necks. When the water temperature cools again in the fall, we go back to clams."

As the crabs migrate north in the Bay and its tributaries, Chris moves his crabbing spots accordingly to locate the crabs. "In early May, I trotline in the Tred Avon River over in Talbot County," he said. "Crabs will get there before they go further north. I'll stay in the Tred Avon until the first of June. In June, I'll move up to the Chester

River following the crabs as they come northward. I'll end up crabbing near Rock Hall for the rest of the season.

"There are lots of restrictions on crabbers now. We have to take off one day each week, either Sunday or Monday. We are limited in the number of female crabs we can catch. We also must quit crabbing by 3:00 p.m. and can't start till an hour before daylight. We have to report our catch to the state each day. If we can't show that 50% or 60% of our income comes from the water, the state will restrict our license even more."

When he works in the Tred Avon, Chris ties his boat to a mooring in the river, preventing the need to trailer the boat each day. "Crabbers are a territorial lot," he said. "When I first went down to the Tred Avon to crab, the local boys gave me a hard time. One time, they sank my boat. Another time, they took the crabbing equipment out of my boat so I couldn't crab. They did things like that for the first seven or eight years I crabbed there. Eventually, they gave up on me and left me alone. I've been crabbing there for twenty years now. I always treat them with respect. I don't get in their way. I respect their lay (the area where the crabber sets his line). We get along OK now.

"The recreational crabbers (noncommercial crabbers who catch crabs for their own consumption), they're the ones that give me a fit. There's 48,000 of them in the state of Maryland. Lots of times they catch over their limit (two bushels). A couple of guys last year were caught with four or five bushels. That's not fair to the commercial guys. Sometimes I'll pull up to a recreational crabbing boat and he'll have a half-dozen bushel baskets onboard. What's he doing with all those baskets? He's only supposed to catch two bushels. He's probably catching as much as he can and then selling the crabs illegally.

"I have to pull up my line by 3:00 p.m. Lots of times there's four or five recreational crabbers waiting to take my lay. I'm allowed to start crabbing at about 4:30 a.m.; recreational guys can't legally start till half-hour before sunrise. I'll often see them out there with their lines set way before I get there. Sometimes I'll go over to them when they are illegally crabbing. I'll tell them that there is a fine of $125 for illegally crabbing with a recreational license. One time, a recreational crabber was out there too early; it was still dark and he ran over my line. He cut my line and I lost 1,000 feet of trotline, as well as the anchor, buoy, and everything else. I went over to him and he denied doing it. He had to have done it; his was the only other boat out there. I probably lost $100 in equipment that day as well as another $100 worth of crabs.

"It's a hard business. You've got to know what you're getting into. There's only about 3,000 commercial crabbers out there now. When I was a kid, there were three times that many. The old-timers don't want all the interference from the state and all the other hardships they have to put up with."

Chris crabs from a 21-foot skiff, powered by a 50-horsepower outboard engine. "I really need to replace that engine," he said. "It's over ten years old and worn out. You figure that it runs about ten hours a day, six days a week and that's a lot of hours. I'd like to get an 80-horsepower to replace it but those motors are expensive. An 80'll cost $7,000 or $8,000."

As the water warms, Chris relocates his crabbing operation further north in the Bay. "Last year, I was crabbing between the Bay Bridge and Kent Narrows and was catching eighteen bushels every day," said Chris. "Then they opened up the flood gates on the Conowingo Dam after Hurricane Irene went through. The spoils from the dam polluted the whole area. It also smothered all the oysters in that end of the Bay. There's not an oyster up there now. We try to tell the DNR what the problems

Chris Skinner's crabbing skiff.

are, but they don't listen. The day after the flood gates were opened, I caught twelve bushels. The next day, I caught six, and the day after that, I only caught three bushels. The crabs all left the area; the water was that polluted. I'm really concerned about that dam. It is getting older and the silt is backing up behind it and there is no place for it to go. When that dam breaks, it'll be the end of the Chesapeake Bay. No living creatures will survive that. It's that serious."

In spite of the frustration of crabbing, there are times when events occur that make the effort memorable. "Nowadays, we use a hydraulic wheel to bring in our lines when we finish crabbing," stated Chris. "Years ago we had to pull them in by hand. One day, I was pulling in my line (by hand) and I noticed a great big old Jimmy (monster crab) hanging onto a bait. As it got closer to the boat, I decided to go after him. I got the net and bent over so I could reach him. I bent over so far that I fell out of the boat. I got back into the boat real quick, hoping nobody saw me. I didn't lose a thing. My glasses were still on my face, but my cap fell off. I went back later and found it floating on top of the water."

Eventually, Chris works himself up to the mouth of the Chester River. "I crab near Eastern Neck Island, not far from Rock Hall," he said. "I've crabbed in that spot since I was a kid. I'll stay there for the rest of the season." Chris is hopeful that the ample supply of crabs continues. "With the exception of a couple of years, the crab supply has held steady for the last twenty or twenty-five years," he said.

"Crabbing is the only hope for the waterman. I'm worried that the supply will not always be there though. There are many more skates (a ray-like fish) in the Bay than I can remember. Those skates swim around in the shallows where the grass beds are and where baby crabs and other animals live. They scoop up whatever is there. Nothing has a chance when the skates get here. Grass beds are like incubators for immature animals. It's a shame. The state blamed swan for pulling up the grasses a few years ago. They got rid of a good many of them at that time. I don't think it was the swan at all, I think it was skates."

Chris refuses to utilize the latest technology for trotlining. "A lot of commercial guys now use dippers when they crab," Chris stated. "Instead of hand-dipping the crab off the line like I do, dippers automatically do it for the crabber. As the boat travels the length of the line, the crabs are forced into the dipper and end up being dragged through the water in a sack for 1,500 or 2,000 feet until the waterman reaches the end of his line. I think dippers drown a lot of crabs as they are forced through the water. Those that don't drown are weaker than hand-dipped crabs. One thing those guys do is go down their lines too fast. If they'd slow down, it'd be much better for the crabs. The crabs I catch by hand-dipping can live for three or four days in a cold box after they're caught. Those that are caught in dippers only last a day or so. The boys who use dippers might lose up to half their catch due to dead loss. I'm not into killing those crabs like that.

"The boys in Rock Hall are so concerned about dippers that they say they are going to the legislature to have the practice outlawed. Because I hand dip, I've had a lot of buyers begging me to sell to them. It tears me up when I see one of those dippers in use."

Chris lives a lifestyle that goes back many generations. "It's like living off the land," he said. "It's getting harder and harder to make a living. I keep doing what I do because of the thrill and challenge of this way of life. It's a rush when I catch something when I check my traps or run down the trotline. There is just too much development, pollution, and erosion. There used to be an island in the middle of the river named Chase Island. It was twelve acres at one time, now it is gone entirely. I trapped a marsh that was forty acres at one time. Now that marsh is down to half that size.

"I feel like I was born a hundred years too late. I should've lived back when wildlife was plentiful. I've got another twenty years in front of me. I don't know what the future will hold. Right now, I just go from day to day and keep hoping things will be okay in the future. Mine is probably the last generation of fishermen and trappers. If things don't change, I don't think the Bay will be productive enough to support another generation. It will probably never improve enough to be as productive as it once was.

"The Bay really could be saved. It is not so bad right now that this couldn't happen, but it would take massive amounts of money and a massive effort. I don't think the politicians and policy makers are willing to make the sacrifices necessary to make it happen.

"I really think that watermen are the true scientists, as far as the Chesapeake is concerned. We're out there every day, observing and comparing how we're doing with how we have done in past years, but we don't get any respect from state officials. Our opinions don't count. The government is out of synch. When the watermen are gone, there won't be any more Chesapeake Bay. When the animals in the Bay die out, humans are done for. When the Bay is no longer productive, there won't be any healthy water to drink or crops to eat. Everything will collapse. If the politicians don't step up, we are all doomed.

"I always thought that if we took care of the environment, it would always be there for us, but now I have my doubts. It seems like we don't care enough about our natural environment. I have doubts that the Bay'll ever come back. I really hope I'm wrong about this. I hope it'll be productive for many more years to come. It'd be a crying shame if we didn't fix it while we had the chance."

CHAPTER FOUR

Clarence Marshall

Clarence Marshall sits in his family room overlooking a tributary of Harris Creek. He speaks longingly about the days when he plied the Chesapeake in his workboats. A lifelong resident of Maryland's Eastern Shore, he is easy to laugh and pleasant. He enjoys reminiscing about his experiences on the Chesapeake.

The 85-year-old Marshall lives within a stone's throw of the house where he was born. "I was born just on the other side of that creek over there," the affable Marshall pointed. "My father was Herman Marshall; he did a little carpentry and also worked on the water. My grandfather was a farmer and he also worked on the water. His name was Charles Marshall. His farm was very small, only about twenty-five acres or so. Grandfather thrashed wheat over on Poplar Island for many years. His thrashing machine (used to separate wheat from the stalk) was powered by steam. The machine also packed wheat into bags. Later, the bags would be sent to Baltimore on freight boats. After he no longer used his thrashing machine on the island, it was abandoned. About ten years ago, erosion caused it to wash into the Chesapeake."

Once containing over 2,000 acres, Poplar Island was inhabited as far back as the 1600s. About three miles from the mainland, by 1880 a town named Valliant was located on the island. Approximately one hundred people resided in the town in those days. In addition to homes, a post office, school, church, and sawmill were part of the community. The sawmill was used to cut trees along the shoreline. Without trees to lessen the effects of erosion, the shoreline began to recede. The relentless Chesapeake, with its enormous appetite, quickly swallowed up much of the island and, in 1920, the Governor of Maryland issued a decree that all residents of Poplar Island should vacate. The island has not been populated by humans since.

Another Chesapeake island that was significant to Clarence was Sharp's Island. Located near the mouth of the Choptank River, not far from the shores of Tilghman Island, there was a gravel pit on the island. "When I was a kid, we used to tow a skiff over there and

44

load it with gravel from a gravel pit," he said. "We'd load that old skiff with gravel until it was just barely afloat. The pit was located on the eastern side of the island. It was a natural gravel pit, not man-made. Lots of people got their gravel from there."

Sharp's Island was once over 1,000 acres. By the nineteenth century, the island was receding at the rate of one hundred feet per year. By 1880, the island had shrunk to seven hundred acres. Today, the island is beneath the waters of the Chesapeake Bay. Once owned by Peter Sharp, a physician, and two partners, he gave the island his name in the seventeenth century. The place was used for farming and raising livestock. Future owners would utilize the island in a similar fashion for many years. In 1813, as the British invaded the Chesapeake, they landed on the island and seized all the livestock. There was some speculation that the owner at the time was a British sympathizer and secretly received payment for the livestock he lost.

In the late 1800s, the island was purchased by a shoe and boot manufacturing executive from Baltimore. An elaborate, three-story hotel was erected on the property and a long pier was driven in anticipation of becoming a stop for steamboats that plied the Bay. The owner envisioned the island as a luxurious vacation spot where visitors from the city could relax and refresh themselves with the cooling Chesapeake breezes. Steamboats failed to land at the island and tourists were in short supply. The hotel languished and was ultimately used only by employees of the shoe and boot company. In 1917, the ill-fated hotel mysteriously burned to the ground. Sharp's Island was eventually used by campers as they hunted and fished in the area. By the 1930s, the island had been reduced to ten acres. A few years later, it vanished altogether.

Today, only a lighthouse marks the spot where Sharp's Island once stood. The lighthouse, a caisson style, lists fifteen to twenty degrees as the result of heavy ice flows that prevailed in the area in the 1970s. To date, Sharp's Island Light is the only caisson structure that has ever veered from its original placement.

Like his father before him, Clarence's father also thrashed wheat. Unlike his father, however, Clarence's dad worked on the mainland. "Dad's thrasher was hooked to a Case tractor by a long belt," laughed Clarence. "The belt powered the thrashing machine and, when I was twelve, my job was to sit on top of the tractor while dad ran the thrasher. If the thrashing machine jammed, he'd yell at me to throw the tractor out of gear so he could fix the problem. I spent many hours on that old Case." The elder Marshall also tonged for oysters in the creeks and rivers that surrounded his home. "I'd go with him when I wasn't in school," Clarence said.

When he was fourteen, Clarence began working summers in a tomato cannery. His job was loading empty cans on a chute during the initial stages of the canning process. Later, he became a mechanic's helper, working on the machinery. He did this for four or five years during summer vacations. "There were canning factories all over the Eastern Shore in those days," he said. "It seemed like every county was loaded with small canneries. Those were the days before the huge, big-name packers."

Clarence bought a 28-foot tuck stern workboat a couple of years later. He paid $175 for the boat and used her for crabbing. "That old boat leaked really badly," Clarence smiled. "I'd work a while, stop and pump her out; work a while longer, stop and pump her again. That would go on like that all day long. She had a one-cylinder Palmer engine in her. That was a great old motor. You'd go along and that engine would just go 'Pop, Pop, Pop' as it ran. I'd like to have one of those engines today just to fiddle with now and then."

Clarence explained that there was an abundance of grass (submerged aquatic vegetation) in the creeks and rivers. "The grass in this creek was so thick that you could almost walk on it," Clarence said sadly. "My, how things have changed. You can't find any grass here now."

Like most watermen at that time, Clarence caught crabs by trotlining. He would set two trotlines, each nearing a quarter-mile in length. "I didn't go oystering in those days," he stated. "I was afraid to stand on the washboards of a boat because I was prone to blackout spells and I didn't trust myself to stand on the gunnels of a rocking boat. I remember one day, when I was in high school, I blacked out on the athletic field. When I came to, I was lying in a ditch and a group of girls were standing over me staring down at me."

Clarence attended school in the town of Wittman. "There was a school there that had grades one through four," he said. "After elementary school, I went to St. Michaels for middle and high school. I played a lot of sports. Because of soccer, I have a knee replacement today. Soccer was my main sport. I played for the St. Michaels High School team. We'd go all over the county playing other schools. It seemed like every little town in those days had a high school. We'd get our soccer shoes from England. The toes in those shoes were just as hard as steel. When you got kicked by one of those shoes, you really felt it."

In 1945, Clarence graduated from high school. "I couldn't get into the military because of my blackout spells," he said. "I also had a back injury. I got married the same year that I graduated. My wife, Betty, and I have been married now for sixty-eight years and have a son, Ted, who retired from the United States Postal Service."

Clarence and his wife also have a grandson, Aaron, and two great-grandchildren, Josh and Hannah. "I own the building where the Wittman Post Office is located," said Clarence. "Betty was the Postmaster there for nearly thirty years before she retired."

The Chesapeake Bay eventually became a source for soft-shelled clams called maninose or white clams. These clams grew to approximately five inches in length and were found about a foot beneath the bottom of the Bay. In New England, a market existed for the very thin, fragile shelled bivalve. Entrepreneurs from New England came to the Chesapeake, opened processing factories, and enlisted the aid of local watermen to provide them with clams. Kent Island became one of the hotspots for the clamming industry in the Chesapeake.

Eventually, Clarence began clamming in his leaky 28-foot boat. "I would set out an anchor on the shore and, with the engine in gear, maneuver the boat back and forth as far as the anchor line would allow it to go," he said. "The propeller would dig a hole in the bottom and blow the sand up in a mound behind the boat. I'd stop the engine and, when the water cleared, jump in the water with a bow net (crab net-like) and collect the clams that had been washed from the bottom. I'd sell the clams to crabbers in the spring, from March through June. They used the clams to bait their eel traps. Then, they used the eels they caught to bait their trotlines."

Clarence explained that there was very little local market for clams where he lived in those days. "Over on Kent Island, clamming was starting to catch on and there were at least four clammers over there," he stated. "They used a different method to catch their clams. They would anchor their boats near shore like I did, but instead of dipping them up with a net, they'd set up a gill net behind the boat and blow the clams into it. Afterwards, they'd have to haul the net aboard. That net would be very heavy by the time it was loaded with clams and everything else that was on the bottom."

In April 1952, Clarence and another clammer, Owen Haddaway, joined forces. "Owen and I went up to Harry Evans Sr.'s foundry in Easton and he and Ford Secrease welded a clam rig for us," Clarence said. "We made a conveyor belt and attached it between two boards that were about twelve inches wide and sixteen feet long. We bolted angle irons onto the boards so that the chain on the conveyor belt would slide on it. On the end of the boards, we attached a four-inch water pump. We'd let the conveyor reach down to the bottom and the water pump would blow the clams onto the belt. We operated the belt with a hand crank. We cranked the clams to the surface and picked off the ones we wanted and the others fell back into the water. We'd get $10 a bushel for our clams, and most days we'd catch about thirty bushels in the Miles River. That was good money back in the '50s."

Eventually, watermen connected a small, air-cooled engine with a reduction gear to eliminate hand cranking. "We tried seven different rigs before we came up with that system," said Clarence. "Owen perfected the system we used for connecting the motor to the belt."

Clarence moored his boat in the St. Michaels harbor in those days. He tied up in front of a house behind what is now the Crab Claw restaurant. The house was owned by a former state senator named Richard S. Dodson, who had represented Talbot County in the statehouse from 1910 until 1914 and again from 1935 until 1939.

"Senator Dodson was a great old guy," said Clarence. "He must've been ninety years old then and he lived alone. He stayed mostly on the second floor of the house. He had two TV sets and they were always turned on. That way he could go from one room to another and not miss anything from the program he was watching. A lady lived on the first floor of his house. She cleaned and cooked for him."

Dodson, according to Clarence, was extremely conservative. Most days he would dress in shirt, coat, and tie, even in the heat of summer. One hot summer day Clarence was working on his boat and had removed his shirt. "It was very hot, it must've been close to one hundred degrees," he said. "I looked up and Mr. Dodson had come down to the boat. He was dressed in a coat and tie and he had on a hat. 'Why don't you put a shirt on?' he suggested. I put my shirt back on and he went on his way. Another time, a sailboat came in and tied alongside his property. On the bow of the boat was a girl in a bikini. He yelled down from his second-story porch and told the couple, 'If you're going to tie up here, you've got to pay me wharfage. By the way young girl, why don't you go down in the cabin and put some clothes on?'"

In 1954, Hurricane Hazel whirled through the area. "When that hurricane went through, the storm surge was so great that my boat floated over the bulkhead and landed near the senator's front porch," Clarence stated. "I tied my boat to his porch railing and, as the tide receded, another fellow and I pushed and pulled and were finally able to get her back in her slip."

Clarence explained that the Senator often seemed lonely. "Many times, after I came in from a day's work in the boat, he'd ask me to come upstairs and sit with him," he recalled. "We'd just sit around and talk about the old days. Sometimes, we'd talk for a couple of hours or more. He was really a nice man."

According to Clarence, Mr. Dodson had owned lots of property around St. Michaels. He owned a great deal of the downtown area and was the founder of one of the local banks. The property where he lived stretched from what is now the Crab Claw restaurant to the wooden bridge that connects the peninsula to Cherry Street. When it was time to collect rent for Clarence's boat slip, Dodson would lower a bucket down from the second-story porch. After the money was placed in the bucket, he would pull it back up to the place where he was standing, write a receipt, and lower it back down. He attempted to get Clarence to buy the land where the Crab Claw is presently located.

"He said he'd take $5,000 for the property," Clarence explained. "He told me that the property would be worth a lot of money someday. He was right! I should've bought the property, but I was very busy in those days clamming and trying to make a living. Eventually, Bill Jones' father bought the property. He only paid $4,000 for it."

The former senator had been raised outside of St. Michaels on a farm named Maiden Point Farm. His father had once owned Herring Island, near the mouth of the Wye River.

Senator Dodson's father, Richard S. Dodson, was awarded a patent for Herring Island on May 13, 1871. At that time, the island was 4-1/2 acres in size. Presumably, he used the island to raise crops and, possibly, livestock. It is unlikely that he resided on the island. The island eventually succumbed to the ravages of erosion. Today, only a shoal marks the area where the island once stood.

According to Clarence, there was little market locally for clams. "Through my contacts with Kent Island clammers, I found out there was a market in New York," he said. "There were three buyers up there and I made some contacts and eventually began sending my clams there. They were shipped up there by way of the Service Trucking Company out of Federalsburg. Later, we sold to a guy in New Jersey."

Fletcher Hanks, formerly of Oxford, is widely credited with inventing the hydraulic clam rig. "He was about a year ahead of Owen and me," said Clarence. "One big difference in our rig and Fletcher's was that his required three engines to operate. Ours only needed one; a rebuilt flathead Ford engine that was hooked up to the water pump. Fletcher had bought a patent from a guy in New York named Hayden. He worked on the rig and perfected it. I knew there was no need to try and get a patent because Fletcher already had one."

One day, as Marshall was working his clam rig, a boat approached and pulled alongside. "A guy from Kent Island, named Thomas, was aboard the boat and he asked if he could look at my rig," Clarence explained. "I told him that would be all right and pulled the rig up so he could see it. The man took lots of pictures and went on his way. Later, I saw the man at a meeting and he said, 'I can't understand why in the world you pulled up that rig and let me take pictures of it. I'd never have done that.' I explained that it appeared that the state was trying to stop us from clamming and I thought that we needed more clammers out there. If our numbers were sufficient, we'd have some influence in Annapolis. State officials were concerned that we would tear up the oyster beds with our hydraulic rigs. I knew we had to get more watermen out there to put pressure on the state so that we could continue to work or the state would run us out of business."

Eventually, Clarence's partner, Owen, contacted their Congressman who arranged for a research vessel from the Corps of Engineers to visit the area where they had been clamming. The crew took soundings all around the area and, finally, concluded that clamming was not detrimental. Even with that, the state maintained pressure, although to a lesser degree.

"We assured state officials that we would not work on the oyster bars," said Clarence. "They finally said that if we agreed not to work the oyster bars they would allow us to continue."

Environmentalists claim that clamming is harmful to the Chesapeake habitat. Many are concerned that clam rigs pull up grasses from the bottom. "Clamming doesn't kill the grasses," said Clarence. "It pulls it up but the grass that is pulled up reseeds itself in other areas. The grass that is left will eventually grow again. Doubleheads (skates) disturb an awful lot of the grasses that are left. They're after clams and small oysters and they dig up the bottom looking for them. There are literally thousands of them out there. They are more numerous now than years ago. You can't go anywhere without seeing them rooting around in the shallows and plowing up the bottom. Their numbers aren't controlled. If they were thinned out, a lot of the grasses could be saved. Oysters and clams too for that matter."

When they formed their partnership, Owen and Clarence agreed that one day Clarence would buy out his partner. "Owen came to me and told me it was time for me to buy his share," Clarence continued. "He wanted $500 for his share and I didn't have that kind of money. I asked my father for a loan and he refused. I went to Mr. Sewell and asked him for a loan. Mr. Sewell owned a grocery store in Wittman and he loaned me the money. I paid off Owen with the money from the loan and the next week went back to Mr. Sewell to pay him off. 'You mean you made that kind of money in one week?' he asked. 'Sure, I made that much and more,' I told him. 'I can't charge you any interest,' he said. 'Just give me the $500 and we'll call it square.'"

By then, a factory had been erected on Kent Island to process clams. The business was called, United Shellfish. "They couldn't seem to get enough clams for processing," Clarence said. "Two other clammers and I bought some property at Lowe's Point in 1956 or '57. At one time, it had been the site of a seafood plant named Harrison and Jarboe. We converted the old building for use as a seafood-processing house and eventually had one hundred employees. We named the business The Chesapeake Shellfish Company. Each of us had two boats that we used for clamming. My boats were forty feet long; one was named *Betty* and the other *Betsy*. They were both named after my wife. In addition to the clams we caught, we also bought clams from other clammers. We set up the building in three sections. One section was used for crabs and another for oysters. The third was used for clams. We also shedded soft crabs there. We'd work clams year-round, crabs in the summer, and oysters in winter. As the oyster population declined, we eventually stopped processing oysters. We had as many as sixty or seventy oyster shuckers working at one time."

In addition to the seafood operation, Lowe's Wharf had a few slips that were used to moor boats. "It was bleak there, especially when a northwest wind blew," said Clarence. "Billy Shores was the caretaker on Poplar Island and kept his boat at the wharf. He also stored some things in one of our buildings. We didn't charge him anything for the use of the place and he let us go over to the island and hunt waterfowl in winters."

Lowe's Wharf had once been a thriving steamboat landing. Served by steamers out of Baltimore and belonging to the Tolchester Line, steamboats landed at Lowe's Wharf four times each week.

Clarence and his partner sold their clams to United Shellfish. "United Shellfish controlled the prices," he said. "They kept cutting the prices they were paying us for clams. The clam supply was also dwindling. There were less and less clams to be caught. Overfishing was one of the primary reasons, I'm sure."

In 1960, Clarence sold his share of the business and the same year bought a 56-foot buyboat named *Stork* from Captain Herman Thomas and his brother on Kent Island. The pair would eventually open the Fisherman's Inn restaurant on Kent Narrows. The *Stork* had been built in Cambridge. "The boat had a Chrysler marine engine in her," said Clarence. "The engine had a V-drive and looked like it was put in the boat backwards. In most buyboats, the cabin was near the stern of the boat, but the *Stork's* cabin was in the front of the boat. She was wide-open behind the cabin. That's where the cargo was stored. She was sixteen feet wide and had lots of flare in her bow. This allowed her to go through some big seas without worry."

Clarence used the boat to buy oysters. He would go to the oyster grounds, anchor, and wait until the tongers and skipjacks finished their work for the day. They would pull alongside the *Stork*, unload their catch, and collect their money. Thereafter, Clarence would take the oysters to a processing house. The boat could hold eight hundred to nine hundred bushels of oysters. "Sometimes we'd also load oysters on trucks and take them as far away as Virginia, to a Campbell's® Soup plant," Clarence said. "We also delivered them to plants along the Nanticoke River."

Bad weather was not unknown to Clarence as he transited the Bay. "One time my brother and I were coming up the Bay with a load of seed oysters (used to populate

Buyboat *Stork. Courtesy of Clarence Marshall.*

oyster beds) in the *Stork* and the weather turned sour," he explained. "We were traveling at night and the Bay had been slick ca'am to that point. About midnight, as we got off the Little Choptank River, the wind hit us at fifty miles per hour or more. The *Stork* was burying her bow in the waves and spray was being thrown all over the boat. We ran for the western shore. We thought the high cliffs over there would give us some shelter from the storm. We anchored in the lee of the high cliffs there and waited till the storm blew out. It was 2 a.m. before the storm passed over and we were able to again head toward home. We finally got home during the early morning hours. After we got home, I had to go out to my shop and weld something that had broken on the boat so I could work the next day."

One very chilly winter evening, about twenty-five years ago, the *Stork* sank at the dock as a hurricane blew through the area. "By then, she was getting kind of loose, so, after we got her floating again, I built a deck across the cargo space," Clarence said. "This stiffened her up a bit and made her more efficient for hauling seed oysters. The government loaned us money to repair the boat after the hurricane." Clarence sold the *Stork* in the 1980s to a man on Tilghman Island. By then, he had installed a diesel engine in the boat. "We had put a four-cylinder Cummins in her," Clarence stated. "She wasn't very fast. She'd only make about six or eight knots."

After selling the *Stork*, Clarence bought a boat he named *Hannah* after his great granddaughter. *Hannah* was forty feet long with a beam of thirteen feet. "She was built in St. Michaels by one of the Spurry boys," he said. "She was fiberglass over plywood."

Clarence used the boat to crab in the creeks and rivers that surrounded his home. His work was more hobby than necessity. "One day, I caught fifty bushels of crabs before 11:30 in the morning," he said. "I was crabbing in the Miles River then and it was the fall. I had two lines out, but the crabs were so numerous that I only had time to use one of them. The crabs were so plentiful that they were hanging on the baits in clumps. They looked like bunches of grapes. I had trouble picking them off the line."

Every day that Clarence went out, he'd notice that a young waterman would set his line alongside his. "One day I asked him why he was laying so close to me," said Clarence. "He answered, 'Mr. Marshall, why don't you get off the water and go home and retire?' I was about seventy-five years old at the time and I guess he would lay near me to help if I got into trouble. It wasn't long before I took his advice and retired."

Clarence now owns a seventeen-foot, outboard-powered boat that he uses for fishing. "I don't get to go fishing as much as I'd like," he said. "Maybe next year I'll use the boat more."

About ten years ago, Clarence began wildlife carving. "I took lessons from Ed and Esther Burns during most of the years I carved," he explained. "They were world-class. Ed did the carving and Esther painted. That's all they did for a living. They traveled around the country selling their carvings. They went to the southern states and all over. One time, a guy in Texas bought just about every carving they had."

The Burns' displayed their work in Easton, at the Waterfowl Festival that is held in November of each year. "You've really got to be good to have your work shown there," said Clarence. "You have to be invited to display at that show."

Clarence explained that he really likes the carvings of French Canadians from Louisiana. "They display every year at the Waterfowl Festival and their work is excellent,"

Wildlife carvings by Clarence Marshall.

Clarence smiled. "The birds they carve look so real that you expect them to stand up and fly away."

Clarence has completed about fifteen carvings. "I sold three of them," he said. "Each carving took about six months to complete. Painting takes hours and hours. I use acrylic paint, but others use oils. Acrylics dry faster and they are easier to work with. Before the carving is painted, a sealer coat has to be put on. About the only thing that isn't carved are the eyes. We buy those and glue them in."

Clarence displayed his work at two competitions. In York, Pennsylvania, he attended the Pennsylvania Wildlife Art Festival in 1985. He won ribbons for second place novice and three first-place ribbons for the array of carvings he entered. He also won the "Best in Show" award for the decorative novice class. For that award, he carved a cardinal resting on a holly branch. That same year he displayed his work in Ocean City, Maryland, at the Ward Foundation World Championship Wildfowl Carving Competition. In that show, he received an honorable mention in the decorative miniature category. "My grandson also used to carve," Clarence stated. "He was a better carver than I was. He also got an honorable mention at the Ward World Championship show."

After Clarence began carving, he stopped hunting. He'd hunted since childhood and shot lots of geese, ducks, and deer. "I just lost interest in hunting," he said. "I never did eat the game I hunted. I tried to eat goose one time, but it made me sick. Just to smell it cooking made me sick. I only hunted for the sport of it."

Clarence has also built a couple of model boats from scratch. "I built a model of the *Stork*," he said. "It was built just like the real one and had a keel, ribs, and planking. I also built a model of a boat that my son owned. He owned a 42-foot Evans fiberglass boat that he used for crabbing and fishing. I did these models about five years ago."

Clarence Marshall holding model of *Stork*.

The prolific Marshall has also completed some oil paintings. "A cousin of mine, Evelyn Reeser, gave some lessons and I enrolled in her classes," he said. "I did about six paintings right after my carving days ended." Clarence explained that he simply no longer has time to paint, carve, or build models. "I don't know what I do with my time, but it seems like I have less and less of it," he smiled.

An avid Orioles fan, he played baseball quite a bit during his youth. In addition to high school, Clarence played on local sports teams throughout the area.

Concerned with water quality in the Bay, Clarence has strong opinions regarding it. "It seems to me that what is polluting the water is wildfowl and fish," he said. "Take geese, for example, there were thousands of them in this little creek last winter. The year before, there were soy beans planted in that field across the creek. Because of the rain, they weren't able to get into the fields to pick the beans and, when the geese came, they stripped the fields bare. They cleaned it up! They'd sit there all day and mess in the fields and it would run off into the water. Some of the roads around here are just matted with manure from geese. There's a lot of fish out there and they also pollute. We now have record numbers of rockfish in the Bay and many more species migrate here in warmer weather. They all leave droppings all over the Bay's bottom, but you never hear anyone talking about that. It's like the doubleheads; nobody talks about thinning them out."

Clarence is pessimistic about efforts to clean up the Chesapeake. "They'll never clean it up," he said. "I don't care what they do; you can't mess with Mother Nature. I've been here for a lot of years and I know what's going on."

Clarence feels everything about the Bay is cyclical. "When you have lots of fish, you don't have crabs," he said. "When you have lots of crabs, you don't have fish. The fish eat the little crabs. We'd catch a load of fish and there wouldn't be any crabs at all in the area. They are saying now that the fish don't have enough of a food supply. It's because there are so many of them out there. They're starving! You can't find even a bull minnow out there because the perch came in and they eat all the grass shrimp and minnows. The supply just isn't out there anymore. There are lots of things going on now. The Bay is being studied to death, but, in the end, only Mother Nature will dictate the final results."

CHAPTER FIVE

Robert S. Fitzgerald

In the southernmost section of Maryland's Eastern Shore lies the county of Somerset. First settled in 1666, it is among the oldest in the state. Named for Lady Mary Somerset, sister-in-law of Cecil Calvert, the 2nd Lord Baltimore, the county originally stretched from the Chesapeake Bay in the south, northward to a portion of what would eventually become Sussex County in Delaware. This massive area included lands that would ultimately become the Maryland counties of Worcester (1742) and Wicomico (1867).

Today's Somerset is comprised of a series of peninsulas, all terminating in the cool waters of the Chesapeake's Tangier Sound. Barely above sea level, the land is abundant with marsh and wetlands, collectively referred to as tidewater. Five rivers reach inward from the waters of Tangier Sound. The Wicomico River marks the northern boundary of the county while the Pocomoke River anchors the south. Smith Island, Maryland's sole remaining offshore inhabited island, along with a series of low-lying abandoned islands, lay on the western edge of the county.

Situated approximately eight miles from the mainland of the eastern shore and an even farther distance from the western side of the Bay, Smith Island is a unique Chesapeake treasure. First settled during the latter half of the seventeenth century, Smith is an archipelago comprised of three islands separated by a series of narrow waterways. At one time, the island was home to more than eight hundred people; the population has since dwindled to about two hundred.

For the most part, islanders earn their livelihood from the Chesapeake Bay. Until recently, the waters surrounding the island provided a seemingly endless supply of oysters, fish, and crabs. As the seafood supply waned due to deteriorating conditions in the Bay, the population decreased and folks relocated to the mainland in search of a more stable livelihood. The remaining island population is, for the most part, of advancing age. Islanders cherish the values of the generations that preceded their own. "This island is all I know," they'll say. "I'll stay here till I breathe my last breath."

The traditions that remain dear to the residents of Smith Island are similarly embraced in other Somerset communities. Isolation, in the early days, spawned a population that developed a unique value system. Many of the customs and habits had their beginnings in Anglo-Saxon Europe. This resulted in a fiercely independent population. Generally, the population has a tremendous respect for the past. From the uniqueness of their Elizabethan accents, reflective of their heritage, to the respect given to their forefathers, a heritage and culture has resulted that is seldom found in other areas of Chesapeake country.

Because Maryland passed a 1649 law entitled An Act of Religious Toleration, a variety of religions were welcomed into the state. Somerset was well known for religious tolerance and several of these religions settled in the county.

In 1659, the state of Virginia passed a law forbidding Quakers from entering. They were seen, by Virginians, as practicing a religion fraught with untruths and falsehoods. Maryland, because of the Religious Toleration Act, welcomed the Quakers and many of them who lived on Virginia's Eastern Shore fled to Somerset County.

In the village of Rehoboth, on the banks of the Pocomoke River, Francis Makemie established Presbyterianism in the United States. Under his influence, the Rehoboth Presbyterian Church was built. It is the oldest Presbyterian Church in the United States. Early Methodism was brought to the county by Francis Asbury, one of the first bishops of the church in the United States. He traveled extensively throughout the Delmarva Peninsula, bringing Methodism to the area.

One of the early converts to Methodism was the Reverend Joshua Thomas. A Somerset native, Thomas was born on Deal Island, but grew up on isolated Tangier Island, a Chesapeake island off the coast of Virginia. A waterman in his early years, Thomas was converted to Methodism and spent the remainder of his life bringing religion to the inhabitants of the many islands that dotted the Chesapeake at that time. Known as The Parson of The Islands, Thomas sailed his thirty-foot log canoe, *Methodist*, from island to island. He is buried beside the Joshua Thomas Chapel on Deal Island.

Robert S. Fitzgerald is a product of this rich culture. His roots in Somerset County reach back to the time when the county was first settled. The youngest of three children, he was born, and continues to live, on land that has been in his family since the seventeenth century. "The property I live on was one of the original land grants from Lord Baltimore," said Bob. "The grant was patented in 1666 and was known as Waller's Adventure. My great-grandmother was a Waller who married a Fitzgerald. They say that all the Wallers in the United States originated here in Somerset County. Waller's Adventure originally included three hundred acres. Approximately 260 of the three hundred acres have never left the family since it was patented. I've managed to buy back almost all of the remaining forty acres, except for five or six. With the help of my brother, I farm the land. It is mostly planted with soy beans.

"Two governors of Maryland have lived within a mile of my place. Governor Levin Widner, the fourteenth governor of Maryland, served during the War of 1812. More recently, Governor Harry Nice, the fiftieth Governor, had a vacation home nearby. Nice was Governor from 1935 until 1939."

The original house that was erected on Waller's Adventure was built in 1710. "There were three brothers who built houses in this area at about the same time," Bob continued. "My grandmother, in about 1890, restructured one of the old houses and made it Victorian in design. When I came to the property to live, I tore down that house and copied the plan of the original house that was across the creek from here.

In the process of excavating, I came across the original footings for the house. I built my present home using the same footprint as the original house. A brick, dated 1710, taken from the ruins of the old house, is in the center of the fireplace chimney in my family room."

Bob has lived in the house for thirty years. "I built the house myself," Bob explained. "My mother helped me and so did my wife, Carolyn. We started building the house in 1972 or '73 and didn't move in until Christmas Eve, 1981. Building the house was quite an experience."

Bob has known Carolyn since second grade. "I remember when she and her family moved here. Their house was not far from ours," he said. "She was a cute little thing with big curls that lined the sides of her face. The curls were so big you could stick your finger in them. I remember seeing her one day sitting on her steps scratching in the soil with a chicken foot. I thought to myself that any girl that could make herself content playing in the soil with a chicken foot must be all right." The couple recently celebrated their fifty-third wedding anniversary.

"Carolyn's great-great-grandfather owned a section of the original land grant, about eighty acres or so," explained Bob. "When we married, we bought it back."

Bob explained that virtually every spot in Somerset County was originally part of a land grant. "Even the marshy areas were included," he said. "One of the largest patents was Almodington. It covered thousands of acres. The estate house is still there. One of the owners of the estate removed the paneling from one of the rooms and, until half dozen years ago when remodeling occurred, it was located in the Museum of Art in New York City. The paneling was returned to Somerset County where it awaits further use."

Another land grant was the 1,400-acre Pomfret Plantation. Fronting on the Annemessex River and Coulbourne Creek, the patent was awarded to William Coulbourne, who served in the seventeenth-century militia as a Brigadier General and was the high sheriff of Somerset County. In 1687, he formulated a peace treaty with the Nanticoke Indians. The existing house on the property dates from 1820 and was built by William Coulbourne VI. The plantation remained in the Coulbourne family until 1921. Currently for sale, it has been reduced to approximately five hundred acres. It may be purchased for a tidy sum approaching five million.

Built in 1663, near the town of Crisfield, Makepiece was another land-grant homesite. It is one of the oldest homes in the state. Built of brick, the house resembles the home built by Bob Fitzgerald, with the exception of its two front doors.

In 1713, the Chase house was built near present-day Princess Anne. It was in this house that Samuel Chase was born. He would go on to become an influential Marylander and a signer of the Declaration of Independence.

"Some of the names of the other land grants were Sweet Wood, Harrington, and Second Purchase," said Bob. "In the 1700s, patents were given for Covington's Vineyard, Covington's Conclusion, Covington's Meadow, Jones Meadow, and Polk's Folly. Polk's Folly was in the middle of a marsh."

Fitzgerald has cultivated an interest in the abandoned towns of Somerset County. "I guess my fascination comes from a variety of reasons," he stated. "Partly my interest comes from my family and the roots we have here. When I was growing up, I heard daddy talk about places like Genngaukin and Pigeon House. These villages completely disappeared years ago. These places have always been interesting to me. As time went on, I started exploring the area where these villages had been located. I guess I've walked over all those areas through the years.

"I can account for approximately ninety homes that have disappeared since 1877 between the towns of Oriole and Dames Quarter alone. I'm a member of the Somerset

County Planning and Zoning Board, so I have access to all the old county maps. I refer to the old maps to locate where villages and houses were once located.

"After reviewing the maps, I visit the area where the villages had been. I still find old foundations and clues to where the houses were located. In March of this year, I went to Genngaukin and found daffodils growing around areas where houses once stood. There were persimmon and apple trees also. You can pretty much tell where the houses were located just by clues like these. There were twenty homes or more in Genngaukin at one time. Some of the homes were moved away. At least one was moved to Salisbury. The last person to live in the village moved away in 1940. I've located about a dozen homes that once were located in Genngaukin and later moved to other areas."

Bob feels that settlers left communities largely because of two reasons. "First, was the availability of reliable transportation," he said. "In the old days, people got around primarily by boat. They lived near creeks and bodies of water that would, eventually, get them to more populated areas. The few roads in existence were in deplorable condition. As roads were improved and people had access to automobiles, they were able to travel outside their immediate surroundings. The other reason, and perhaps it's the major reason, was sea level rise. The low land is washing away. This has been going on for some time. In the last fifty years, I've seen a lot of land disappear because of sea level rise. I've been interested in this since 1984 when I became a board member of the Somerset County Soil Conservation District."

Bob has been very active in Soil Conservation District activities. In addition to his membership on the county conservation district, he was a member of the Maryland Soil Conservation Service for eight years. During his tenure, he held almost every office in that organization. At one time, he was the state representative for the northeastern United States.

"I used to have a lot of interaction with former Lieutenant Governor Kathleen Kennedy Townsend (a member of the John Fitzgerald Kennedy clan)," said Bob. "She used to call me 'cuz.' It broke my heart not to vote for her when she ran for Governor, but I didn't."

Because of sea level rise and degradation due to the effects from it, Bob stated that Somerset County has lost 7,000 acres of tillable land since 1988. "The amount of tillable land that is currently available in the county is less than half what it was just sixty or seventy years ago," he said. "Salt water intrusion from the waters of the Chesapeake is what makes the land no longer viable. When salt water intrudes on the land, it is no good for farming from then on. Because Somerset is barely above sea level, this continues to be a huge problem.

"There's an estate not far from here named Elmwood. Elmwood was the home of my great-grandfather, Thomas Henry Fitzgerald. His father, Elijah Fitzgerald, had relocated to the area from the Eastern Shore of Virginia, in Accomac County. We don't know much about what happened to him or his wife, but we do know that his children were raised by my great-great-uncle, Jesse Fitzgerald. My great-grandfather was just about worked to death by Jesse. He ran away and went to sea. His brother, Henry, also had gone to sea. The brothers were shipwrecked off Cape Hatteras in about 1861 or 1862. His brother drowned, but Thomas survived and returned home. He never went to sea again. He bought Elmwood and lived there from 1862 until his death in 1902. Over at Elmwood, there are places in the fields where nothing grows. That's because salt water from the nearby river got into the soil and rendered it useless.

"Quindocqua, which is adjacent to Marion Station, was another town that was once a vibrant Somerset community. A hundred years ago, Quindocqua had its own church and school. There was even a seafood processing plant there, with a long pier that extended

Manor house at Elmwood.

out into the river. Hurricane Hazel took what remained of the pier and processing plant away in 1954. Locals claim that one of the Vanderbuilts had a hunting lodge near Quindocqua. Sea level rise took it all away. Only the foundation of the lodge remains.

"Pigeon House was a village that sat on the banks of Pigeon House Creek. Pigeon House Creek almost looks like it was hand-dug because it is so straight. When you walk down there, you can see where the citizens built up the banks with slab wood so that horses and wagons could get down to the creek. You find a lot of that around old creeks.

"Pigeon House was originally called Bethel on some of the older maps. Several members of Carolyn's family, the Bozeman's, are buried in the cemetery there. Bozeman, Montana, reportedly took its name from the Bozeman family that originated in Somerset.

"Potato Neck, not far from Fairmount, was another village that is completely gone. The area got its name from the large numbers of potatoes that were grown there. It's all gone because of sea level rise.

"A man told me about a village called Landonville, near Potato Neck and Fairmount. Many of the citizens there worked on the water for a livelihood. During the early part

of the twentieth century, apparently working the water was not very lucrative. Most of the people who lived in the village left and moved to Baltimore, where they worked in shipyards during World War I. They never returned to Somerset County.

"There's a place called Upper Hill, also not far from Fairmount. It's a predominantly black community. Blacks settled there after the Civil War. It was known then as Freetown. There was also a black settlement, called Liberia, located near Quindocqua; it came into being after the Civil War. The church there is still called Liberia Methodist Church.

"Speaking of churches, I don't go near one if I don't have to. I passed by a church and it looked like it was ready to fall down. The sides were sagging and it seemed to be unsafe. Another fellow and I from the Planning and Zoning Commission went into the church to look it over. That evening it snowed about six inches and the roof caved in. I tell everybody that I can't go inside a church because I'm afraid it'll collapse. One time, I went to a candlelight service with Carolyn and when I walked in everybody looked up at the ceiling. I thought to myself, 'That's the greeting I get.'"

One of the Somerset communities became famous as a boat-building center. A number of bugeyes and skipjacks were built in the village of Oriole. Originally named St. Stevens, Oriole took its name from the abundance of nesting Baltimore Orioles in the area. "Benjamin Franklin Laird was a boat-builder in the town and his son was about to be drafted for service in the Civil War," said Bob. "In those days, you could buy your way out of the draft. Benjamin sold his log canoe for $200 and gave the money to the government so that his son didn't have to go to war.

"One of the boats that Laird built was a bugeye named *William B. Tennyson*. The *Tennyson* has survived and is now over to the Calvert Maritime Museum in Solomons, where she was converted to a power boat. She takes visitors for rides on the Patuxent River."

Many folks feel that sea level rise is a myth. These people feel that it is an environmental phenomenon that is cyclical in nature. Bob takes exception to that line of thinking. "Sea level rise can't be denied," he said. "In the past fifteen years or so, it has gotten worse. You don't have to look any farther than the Blackwater Wildlife Refuge, below Cambridge. Since its founding in 1933, the refuge has lost over 7,000 acres. I flew over it a couple of years ago for the first time in ten years. It was amazing to see how much it had changed.

"Experts say that by 2100 most of the town of Crisfield will be gone because of sea level rise. Even now, during some exceptionally high tides, water washes into the town for a quarter-mile or more."

The 74-year-old Fitzgerald is the product of a family that regarded education highly. "My mother was a college graduate," he said. "She encouraged us to get an education. She graduated from what is now Longwood College. She majored in Home Economics there. She never taught; she found that she could make a lot more money raising turkeys than teaching. She graduated in 1921 when teachers were making $300 a year. Even though dad's past is largely a mystery, we do know that he attended business school in Philadelphia. My sister is a retired teacher who graduated from the University of North Carolina. Dad's cousin was also an educator. He served as Superintendent of Schools in Somerset County and also in Caroline County further north on the Shore."

Retired from the Somerset County Public Schools, Bob graduated from nearby Salisbury State College (now Salisbury University). "If you were from Somerset County, in those days people thought you were dumber than hell," he laughed. "I guess there may have been some truth to that, however. Somerset gave away Ocean City and Salisbury and kept Frogeye and Shelltown."

Bob began his teaching career at Deal Island High School, which was connected to the mainland by a bridge. He taught an array of subjects at the school from 1961 until 1966. "I even taught girls' Phys. Ed.," Bob explained. From 1966 until 1971, he taught math at Washington High School in the town of Princess Anne. In 1971, he began a stint as a Vocational Guidance Counselor. In 1973, he was charged with planning the design, building, and curriculum for the J. Millard Tawes Vocational Center. The center opened in 1976 with Bob as its Director. From 1979 until 1981, he was the Supervisor of Secondary Education and, from 1981 until his retirement in 1991, he was the Assistant Superintendent for Administrative Services.

In addition to his many duties caring for his three hundred acres, Bob finds time to indulge in a few hobbies. "I have a collection of about thirty tractors," he said. "I have always been interested in tractors. We've always had them around on the farm. Most of them were Farmall. The first tractor I ever drove was a Farmall F-12 model. I went to an auction one day and bought an F-12; I hadn't seen one in years. I brought it home and got it running and restored it. After getting the F-12, I decided to get an F-20. After that, I bought a 10-20, and then I decided to collect all the letter series. I have an A model and an AN, a B, BN, a C, four or five H's, an M, and super M. I have over thirty now. I just kept on collecting. I'll go out and crank them over from time to time and keep up the tires. I also have two John Deere's in a state of restoration. They are stored in buildings all over the farm. One day, I decided to get one of the tractors running that hadn't been started for about ten years. I worked and worked on that old tractor and finally got it running. Sometimes I wonder why I expended so much effort because it'll probably be another ten years before I start it again."

Bob also has a collection of pick-up trucks. "I own about ten or fifteen Ford pick-up trucks," he stated. "When I was a kid, we always had Fords. When I'd come across an old Ford pick-up at an auction, I'd buy it. It seems like now I'm a lot better at getting them running than finishing the restoration. I'm not too good at completing them. Guess I've become one of those ninety-percenters."

Bob became interested in decoy carving after his retirement. "Carolyn was convinced that I wouldn't have enough to do to fill my time," he said. "So I took up decoy carving. I guess I started doing it to prove to myself that I could. For a long time I collected decoys. I would give them away as Christmas presents. I thought to myself that I could carve a decoy as well as a lot of the ones I collected. There's a decoy over there that I copied from a Ward Brothers (two of the premier waterfowl carvers) decoy. Mine looks just like theirs. I'm pretty good at copying.

"I don't really carve them; I grind and scrape them. I do have a Dremel tool, but I don't even own a carving knife." Bob estimates that he has fashioned about seventy-five decoys over the years. He's never sold any, but he has given some away. "I don't sell anything I have," he laughed. "The only thing I sell are the soybeans growing out there in the field."

In 1968, Bob traveled to the airport in Laurel, Delaware. "A guy took me up in an airplane and I really enjoyed it," Bob said. "I decided to take flying lessons and eleven weeks later I had my pilot's license. Shortly thereafter I bought my first airplane. I had a couple of partners. In 1970, I bought a 1946 Aerocoupe. I had it right out here in the backyard where I restored it. I sold that and bought a Cessna 150 with a partner. In the late '80s, I bought a Cherokee 180. It was a rough-looking plane. It was so rough that I was afraid to fly it. We bought the plane in Easton and the owner flew it down here for my partner and me. We restored the plane and it really came out well. We even replaced the engine. We took lots of day trips. We'd go to Cape May for breakfast, for example. I love to fly over the Bay and look down and see all the changes that continue to take place. Lately, I haven't used the plane as much as I used to. It stays in a hanger in Salisbury. It's a beautiful little airplane. It's never so much as had a drop of rain water on it since we restored it."

Bob has also had motorcycles as well as boats. He has been an avid hunter and fisherman. "I pulled my old boat out of storage a few weeks ago," he smiled. "I bought the boat in 1970; the engine was built in 1968. The boat and engine had been in storage for nine years and were ignored. I pulled that starter cord only two times and the engine started. That's a phenomenal little engine. I launched the boat and ran around the creeks and rivers looking at the damage from the erosion process. It breaks your heart to see it."

Bob and Carolyn enjoy traveling. "Right after our wedding we drove to Niagara Falls," said Fitzgerald. "In 1966, we inadvertently took an elongated trip. We planned a three- or four-day trip to Michigan. When we got there, we decided to go on to Mount Rushmore. At Mount Rushmore, we decided to go on to Yellowstone, and then Idaho and Seattle. From Seattle, we drove south along the coast to San Francisco and Los Angeles, before heading home. We were gone twenty-one days on that trip and our total cost for food and gas was only $420. Since then, we've driven cross-country nine more times. By 1968, we had been in all of the forty-eight mainland states.

"In 1978, Carolyn graduated with an advanced degree from nursing school. We decided to go to Europe as a reward. We've been there about every five years since that first trip. So far we've been in thirty-six European countries. Every trip has been memorable. Five years ago we spent a month in China, Hong Kong, and Tibet. When we were in Ireland, we ran across the Fitzgerald coat of arms. There are two versions. One version has a boar on it while the other has a monkey. The boar symbolizes strength, but the monkey has an interesting story behind it. A Fitzgerald castle caught fire and an infant was trapped in the fire. The family apparently had a monkey as a pet. When the fire was extinguished, neither the infant nor the primate could be found. The family mourned the loss of their daughter. A short time later, the monkey came out of a closet that had not been burned in the fire. In his arms, he was carrying the baby. He had taken it to safety.

"I've driven from Nova Scotia to Vancouver. A couple of years ago I drove to Alaska with a buddy. We drove 11,301 miles on that trip. We've also traveled across Mexico on local buses. Carolyn and I rode buses with chickens and hot, sweaty Mexicans who

Bob Fitzgerald surrounded
by decoys he has carved.

looked at us kind of funny. We almost got into trouble one time on a bus when a drunk got on and started giving us a rough time. That was a little unsettling."

Bob Fitzgerald leads an exciting life. He looks on his homeland with fondness and is proud of his Somerset heritage. "I just love this land," he says. "It's a shame that it can't be preserved for the generations that follow. One of my greatest concerns is that future generations will not have an appreciation and respect for the land. Until recently, we've not been alarmed at the rate the land is leaving us. This has become one of the symbols of our throw-away generation. Hopefully, future generations will be better custodians of the environment than we have been."

Chapter Six

Willy Roe

Willy Roe, Jr. holding a trophy he won in a fishing tournament.

A few generations ago, just shy of 2,000 hardy souls called Tilghman Island home. The majority of these citizens earned a livelihood from the abundance of seafood found in the fertile waters of the nearby Chesapeake Bay. The productive Bay supplied a great deal of the seafood that graced the tables of folks from across the land and beyond. Tilghman Island played a vital role in this endeavor.

For hundreds of years, Tilghman, like all communities on Maryland's Eastern Shore, was relatively isolated. The population has dwindled to seven hundred, many of whom are not native to the island. Many natives, though, continue to cling to the lifestyle of their forefathers. It is a lifestyle that is beautiful in its wholesomeness, its honesty, and its sincerity. It is in this land that William (Willy) Roe, Jr. was blessed to be born.

Born a stone's throw from the Chesapeake on Tilghman, Roe has seen tremendous changes in the Bay and the way of life it inspired. "My family was poor when I was coming up," Willy said. "Everybody on the island was poor back then, it seems. We lived with few modern conveniences. We didn't have electricity or running water in the house until I was a good-sized boy. When I was seven, dad put in an indoor bathroom. Until that time, we used an outhouse. When we got water in the house, there was a hand pump that emptied into the sink. To get water, you had to pump it up from the well with the handle of that pump. That was a lot harder than just turning on a faucet.

"Dad worked on the water all his life. He sold what he caught to the Tilghman Packing Company, where all sorts of seafood was processed. My mother worked there. The Tilghman Packing Company was located on a peninsula of land, almost looked like an island, with a narrow causeway running out to where the buildings were located. At one time, that land had been used as a steamboat landing.

"Because Dad was a waterman, his job changed with the seasons. In the summer, he hauled seine for fish. He was one of the best on the Bay. I started going out fishing with him when I was three or four years old. My grandmother had watched me till I was old enough to go out on the boat with dad. Dad fished at night. We'd leave on the boat about 4 p.m. and dad would fish all night. He could make three hauls in a night. If he hit on lots of fish, only one haul was necessary. He was after a fish called hardheads, or croakers. Those fish made a loud grunting sound. That's how they got their name. I've been out there and, as we passed over a big school of hardheads, you could hear them underneath the boat. That's hard to believe, but it's true. By the time I was eight or nine, I knew enough to be of some help."

The haul seine was essentially a net, approximately half-mile-long with poles on either end and cork floats on the top side. There were weights on the bottom edge to keep the net near the bottom. The seine was set (placed) in a semi-circle by a thirty-foot seine skiff near the shore in shallow water. As the seine skiff narrowed the gap between the two ends of the net, men jumped into the water and manually closed the opening. At that point, the fish that were gathered in the net could not easily escape and the nine-man crew dipped them out of the net. "There were nine haul seine rigs on this island in those days," the affable Roe said. "One time a Tilghman haul seine rig caught seventy-five tons of fish. A guy down to the Potomac once caught 150 tons in one night. The seine that dad had could hold eighteen tons of fish."

By the 1950s, haul seining in the Chesapeake had slumped. Croakers were not plentiful like they had been, and they almost died out altogether. Very few of the fish have been caught since. The elder Roe also used pound nets for fishing. Winter fishing was done by way of drift nets or gill nets.

"When dad fished with pound nets and drift nets, he was after rockfish (striped bass) and perch," Willy said. "He caught a lot of fish using these methods. Back then, gill nets were made from cotton or linen. They required a lot of maintenance. Every day they were used, the nets got weaker and eventually wore out. A lot of the money that dad made from fishing went toward replacing his nets. After World War II, nylon came out and nets were made from that material. Nylon was much better; it was rot-resistant and it stretched. Because of this, different-sized fish could be caught in the same net. Before, the net had to fit the fish you were after. Nylon gill nets would catch twenty-to-one over linen or cotton. Later, dad buried some nylon net out in his garden to see what would happen. He couldn't believe it when he pulled it up and it hadn't rotted — that was his way of testing it.

"Buddy Harrison and I were good friends and from the time we were in elementary school we'd go and set gill nets before we went to school. We were after rockfish. We'd get up early to tend our nets and, when we caught a lot, we'd be late for school. In elementary school, the days when we were late we'd just go to our rooms and sit down at our desks. The teacher knew what we were doing and didn't say anything. When we got old enough to go to St. Michaels and the Jr.-Sr. High School, we had to report to the principal when we were late. We told him why we were late and he told us that when we were late we had to bring two rockfish to school and put them in the refrigerator in his office. We did that and had no problems with being late after that."

Tilghman was overrun with rats when Willy was a boy. "During World War II, when I was about ten, I had a little dog and that dog was real good at catching rats," Willy explained. "Every family had gardens and chickens. Some raised hogs and horses. My mother raised chickens and had a brooder house and sold eggs to people. People used to come and borrow my dog when the rats became a problem. My dog hunted rats over to the elementary school, in stores, and also in homes; he went all over the island.

"Behind the school was a big place on the Bay side that had a couple of horses and a corn crib. The people who lived there had only been there about a year when they started having problems with rats. I took my dog over there one day and he caught lots of them. The lady who lived there took a liking to my dog after that and, often, would let him come inside the house and stay the night. Our house was only a block or so away, so we weren't worried. A couple of times when I went over there, I noticed that they had a lot of telescopes set up around their property. A short while later, I missed my dog. He hadn't come home for several days. I was down at the drugstore and the lady behind the counter asked me if I had sold my dog. I told her I hadn't, but my dog was missing. She said that the couple who lived behind our house had stopped to say goodbye one night about midnight. She said they were on their way to California and my little dog was in their car. We found out later that the couple were German immigrants who were spies for the German government. They reported every ship that went up or down the Bay. They were eventually caught in California, but I never did get my dog back."

When Willy was ten or twelve, his dad began taking out fishing parties. A woman named Lowenthal went with him every Wednesday during fishing season. She came on Wednesdays for a number of years to fish with the senior Roe. Mrs. Lowenthal owned a popular chain of pharmacies at the time. Often, she would bring personnel from her stores for a day on the water. When Mrs. Lowenthal drove down to the boat, she towed a trailer behind her car. That was the only trailer Willy ever saw on Tilghman in those days.

"I was the bait boy [removed fish from lines and rebaited hooks] during a lot of those trips," Willy stated. "Dad would take Mrs. Lowenthal down to the mouth of the Choptank River and they'd catch three hundred to five hundred hardheads each trip. He'd put the fish in iced-down crab barrels. She wanted to catch every fish that she could. She'd want to stay out there and fish long after the barrels were full. After filling the barrels, dad wanted to go in. He'd get me aside and tell me to throw the rest of the bait overboard so we could go on home. It seemed like every time she came, she'd bring more and more bait. I had a job to get rid of it. I think she must've been selling all those fish she caught."

Before the war, the supply of oysters in the Bay had dwindled. Like many island men, Willy's dad went to Baltimore and worked in shipyards building liberty ships for the military. He took his boat there and lived on it during the week. On weekends he came home. After the war, oysters became plentiful once again.

Willy was a good baseball player. When he was twelve years old, he played in a men's league. "I was a good hitter," Willy stated. "I had a good eye…I could see the ball coming toward me and could tell by the way it was spinning whether it would curve or just what it was going to do. The baseball coach at the school, Mr. Ernie Lowango, told me that I couldn't legally play until I got into the ninth grade, but he would let me practice with the team anyway.

"I was playing an inter-squad game one day and a member of the team, he was a senior, got a hit and came around to third base where I was playing and spiked me in the ankle. He was jealous that a twelve-year-old was playing with the high school boys. The next day, Mr. Lowango noticed me hobbling around and told me to come into his office. 'Where are your spikes?' he asked me. I told him they were in my locker and he told me to get them and bring them to him. I brought them to him and he sat at his desk and filed each spike until it was as sharp as a razor, and then he handed them back to me and told me to spike the boy who had spiked me the day before. In a couple of days, we had another inter-squad game and I got a hit and ended up on first base. The boy who spiked me was playing second base. The next player at bat got a hit and I ran down there and slid into the boy who had spiked me. I planted both feet in his chest. Blood spurted out through his shirt; it was a mess. The next day, Mr. Lowango saw me and said, 'I told you to spike the boy, not kill him.'

"Mr. Lowango told me I had the best hitting eye he'd ever seen. He said that he would bend the rules and let me play with the team on one condition — he told me that I could play, but if I ever struck out I wouldn't play the next game. I never did strike out after that. If I had two strikes, I'd just meet the ball so I didn't strike out.

"One day, when I was fourteen, some scouts from the New York Giants and the Brooklyn Dodgers came down here and watched me play. They came over to the house and talked to my parents and to me. They told me I had a good chance to make it in professional ball.

"When I was fifteen and in the tenth grade, I decided to quit school. The very last game I played for St. Michaels was up to Centreville. I got four hits that day and won the game for our team. I was really improving. I had nine triples that year and was hitting the ball harder than ever. I had played in a teenaged league and Mr. Lowango had taught me how to break my wrists when swinging to give me more power. I led the league in stolen bases that year; I had thirty-eight for the season. Mr. Lowango was the best coach I ever had; he taught me a lot.

"When I quit school, there was only about three weeks left before the school year ended. I didn't even go back to pick up my report card. I went fishing with dad. In the fall, a truant officer came to my house and tried to get me to go back to school. Mom pleaded with me to go back; she cried and everything, but I was making money fishing.

"After their first visit, the scouts came again for the next two years. I always wondered how things would have worked out if I'd continued to play ball. I always wondered if I would have made it as a professional baseball player. As I think back on it, I made lots of money commercial fishing. A commercial fisherman, in those days, could make a lot more money than a professional ball player. Just the opposite is true today.

"Tilghman Islanders always enjoyed playing practical jokes on each other back then, especially on us kids. There was no such thing on the island as TV or anything like that. We made our own fun. It got so that joking around was really part of the way of life on the island. I remember one time when a couple of friends and I went to Easton to the Avalon Movie Theatre. We took a bag with us and in the bag we put about six live crabs. We put those crabs all around the theater. We put one on a seat and that crab didn't crawl off. A woman and man came in and the lady sat in the seat, right on top of the crab. She took off her coat and put it on the seat before she sat down and every time she moved that crab would bite her. We were standing in the back of the theatre giggling at what we saw. Every time the crab would bite her she'd let out a scream. The man that was with her thought it was funny and started laughing. It created a terrible scene. The theater people sent for the cops and they came and threw all of us out of the place. We had some funny experiences, that's for sure."

After ending his formal education, Willy continued fishing with his dad. "Dad had a brand new boat built. She was forty-five feet long and had a twelve-foot beam. The first year I fished with him was the first year he tried using nylon gill nets. We fished all over the Bay, from the headwaters up north down to the Potomac. We started fishing right after Christmas and fished up until June. We fished seven days a week and lived aboard the boat. It was a rough life living on the boat. I thought to myself, 'What have I done? My buddies are all warm back in school and here I am out here.' There were lots of fish that year and we made lots of money. After I started making money, I never looked back and didn't think about school anymore. While I was down on the Potomac, I saved $4,000. I used $1,000 of it to buy a brand new pickup truck. There were only two or three pickups on the whole island in those days.

"One time dad was over to Sandy Point, not far from the state park. He knew there was a school of fish up there, but they were a ways offshore. He went up there and stayed a week or more. I wasn't with him that time, but when he came home on the weekend he told me that if that school comes ashore he'd make a year's wages right there. To that point, it had been a lean year for dad, one of the worst he'd ever had.

"He went back and started fishing at midnight and those fish came inshore. I forget how many tons of fish he caught, but he had so many that he had to send word for more boats to come up to haul them home. He made his year's work and paid all his expenses with that one haul. After he got the fish out of the nets, he told the crew that he was done fishing. The crew said, 'Mr. Will, you can't quit now.' Dad told them that he had promised his God that if he ever made enough money to get out of the hole, that would be it. He never fished again after that."

In the 1950s, an island near the mouth of the Choptank River was used by the U. S. Navy for target practice. Planes from the Patuxent Naval Air Station would fly across the Bay and either release bombs or fire on Sharp's Island. Between the bombing, shelling, and erosion, the island had been reduced to five acres. At one time, however, the island sheltered an entire community.

Willy's grandfather, Howard Sinclair, was the last baby to have been born on the island. "Grandfather was a widower and living with my parents by then," said Willy. "The local newspaper found out about him being the last baby born on the island and thought it would be a good idea to have a picture of him standing on the island. Dad agreed to take grandfather and a photographer to the island for the picture later when spring came.

"There was a hard freeze for a week or so about then. When it thawed, dad and I and another boy went net fishing. Dad always steered down to the fishing area and, on the way home, we would steer while he took a nap. After we had fished, we were headed home and came upon beach-cove buoy, which was not far from Sharp's Island. I was steering and I couldn't see Sharp's Island to save my life. We called dad and he said to steer westward and we'd miss it all right. I did as he said, but I still couldn't find the island. It turned out that the ice had taken what was left of the island away. It was totally gone — underwater. We went home and told grandfather that he wouldn't have to go and get his picture taken cause no island existed."

In January 1955, Willy got married and two weeks later the couple bought their first house. "I went to the bank to borrow the money and the man told me that I'd need somebody to sign for me 'cause I was so young," said Willy. "Dad said he'd co-sign the loan. It was winter and we were froze-up and couldn't get out fishing. The ice broke up on a Saturday and I went out drift-netting before the loan went through. I made enough money that one day to buy our first home. I made $4,800 that day. Fish were plentiful; we got thirty cents a pound for them. We caught mostly rock and perch. We bought a house on Wharf Road for $4,500 and still had $300 left over. Dad had never got that much money for fish in his life. I wasn't the only one to do that. Three or four other guys around here bought their houses with earnings from one night of fishing."

During the warm season, Willy crabbed. "I trotlined and sold the crabs I caught for as little as two cents a pound," he said. "Crabs, in those days, traveled in schools like fish. I've caught as high as seven bushels with one run of the line.

"There wasn't much market around here for crabs in those days. I drove up to New York in my pickup truck and found a market up there. They told me they could take up to one hundred bushels a day and they would give me $7 a bushel for them. They said that I had to get them to New York, though. They also told me about a guy on Kent Island that was bringing clams to New York every day and maybe I could work out something with him. I talked to the Kent Island man and he agreed to haul my crabs on his clam truck. He charged me $2 a bushel. At the time, I had only been getting .80 a bushel here. Even with paying for the freight, I cleared $5 a bushel. I knew, though, I couldn't supply the one hundred bushels that the buyer wanted, so I partnered with Wade Murphy, Sr. Each of us sent fifty bushels every day.

"The road that ran down to the Tilghman Packing Co. had a public landing at the end of it. Wade and I would bring our boats to the landing, meet the truck from Kent Island, and unload our crabs. The second day we unloaded, a sheriff came along and told us we couldn't unload there. He said only farmers could use the landing, not watermen. The next day we tied our boats next to the causeway and unloaded onto the road. Two or three days later, the sheriff came again and told us we couldn't do that because we were blocking the roadway. It turned out that there was a man on the island who owned a lot of property and he wanted to stop us from doing what we were doing.

"A man we knew, Clay Lowrey, owned a place on the water, right on the narrows. We went to see him and he allowed us to unload on his property for $15 a month. A couple of days later, the man who tried to stop our operation went to him and tried to rent his whole place. When Lowrey refused his offer, he had a man follow the truck to New York and he tried to bargain with the owner, saying he could deliver crabs cheaper than he was paying us. The fellow didn't go for his offer. That's how competitive the business was."

Eventually, Willy became part-owner of a pair of skipjacks: the *Martha Lewis* and the *Kathryn*. His partner was a Tilghman man named Russell Dize and they were together for a long time. Dize dredged the *Kathryn* and Willy worked the *Martha Lewis*. The boats were difficult to keep up. They required a lot of maintenance. "I dredged the *Martha* for four or five years; it was the hardest thing I've ever tried to do," he said. "I couldn't keep her up. I'd spend $10,000 a year just trying to keep her up. When I sold her, I hired a band and had a party. That was the happiest day of my life."

Willy sold his boat to a neurosurgeon from Alabama. "He told me he had always wanted to restore one of those old boats," said Willy. "A couple of years later I took him out fishing and he told me that the *Martha Lewis* had caused him to get a divorce. He had spent so much money on her that his wife got disgusted and left him. I told him that if I'd known that was going to happen I never would have sold her to him."

Just prior to Hanks' successful invention of the hydraulic clam rig, many watermen attempted to build their own rigs. Some were using crude rigs of their own design. "I started building a clam rig when I was seventeen years old," said Willy. "My father made me stop building the rig because Fletcher found out about it and threatened to sue him. Because I was underage, Fletcher was going to sue my dad for patent infringement. The rig I started building was never used, but all the parts came in handy later on.

"Later, my father-in-law and I went up to Kent Island and had a clam rig built and went into the clam business. Our rig was superior to the rigs that Fletcher built. Our rig could go straight while Fletcher's couldn't. The belt on his rigs pulled the boat around; it couldn't go straight. His rigs could catch twenty or thirty bushels a day; ours could catch fifty bushels. We'd finish our day's work and be home by 10 a.m. while the others were still out there. We didn't have a very good market for selling clams, but Fletcher did. We dealt with a man who had an oyster processing plant where the Chesapeake Bay Maritime Museum is now located. In the summer; he processed clams, but he didn't have a big market like Fletcher; therefore, he couldn't handle as many clams.

"One day Fletcher called my father-in-law and asked if we could get him twenty bushels the next day. My father-in-law agreed and the next day we went out in the Miles River, near Deepwater Point, and started clamming. We noticed a couple of Fletcher's

Artifacts brought up from bottom of
the Chesapeake Bay while clamming.

boats nearby, but didn't think much about it. As we clammed, we noticed that bubbles would come up from the bottom every now and then. We thought we were hung up on something and pulled up the rig. When the belt came up, there was a diver sitting on the end of it. It was Fletcher — he was down there looking at our rig. He jumped off and swam over to one of his boats and got aboard. Some of the boys that had Fletcher's rigs had started complaining because our rig caught more than theirs.

"Clams were bringing in more money than some of the watermen had ever made. The Bay was loaded with them. In the Miles River, for example, we could catch clams twice a year. In the spring, the clams would be very small, maybe an inch or so, but by November those clams would grow to four or five inches and be market size. Over the winter, the small ones would grow again and we could catch those in early spring. It was the same in all the rivers around here. Clams were everywhere. They'd come back every year. In those early years, there were no catch limits, but the state put limits on us later on.

"I wanted the state to put in a season for clamming, but they refused. We even hired a bus one time and went to Annapolis and testified about having a clam season. The big-money boys from New England apparently had Annapolis in their hip pockets.

"The next year, my father-in-law and I made another rig using the leftover parts from the rig I started building years before. Fletcher sued me and my father-in-law and also others who weren't paying him royalties to use his patent. He sued me for $20,000 for each rig. Back then $20,000 was a lot of money.

"I saw Mr. Clay Lowrey one day and explained that I was being sued by Hanks. He told me to call his son, Orem, who was living across the Bay at Broomes Island. He said that Fletcher was suing him also. He had four or five clam rigs and shucked them down there. I called Orem and he asked me to find out how many were being sued. I found that there were seventeen people on Kent Island who were involved in the suit besides my father-in-law and me. Orem invited all of us over to his house for a meeting. His wife laid out a buffet lunch for us and we drank mint juleps. By the time we left there, we were all a little tight. Orem told us to meet him the next day and we'd all go to Washington and meet with his lawyer. The lawyer told us he would take the case for free. Orem's wife was his secretary and they were good friends. He said that for $1,700 each, for expenses, he would represent us. He made us commit to being available when he needed us and everyone agreed. He said the case would likely drag on for three or four years.

"Our first day in court, I was sitting behind Fletcher and I heard his lawyer ask, 'How in the hell did they ever afford to pay their lawyer?' Eventually, we won the case and Fletcher's patent was useless. It was the late 1950s by then.

"Bill Jones went into the clam business where the Crab Claw Restaurant is now. He sold his clams to New England and the market loosened up for us. After a few years, Russell Dize, Freddy Sadler, and I opened up our own seafood house in McDaniel, where we shucked oysters and clams for the next thirty years. I ran the shucking house while they went out in the boats and brought in clams and oysters.

"The first year was rough. We had seven or eight boats that we were running and we couldn't afford to pay the $30,000 fuel bill that we had accumulated. The second year, we struck clams off Sharp's Island. We could catch thirty bushels in an hour. Our boats would come in loaded with one hundred bushels or more. Sharp's Island really bailed us out. By the end of that year, we had paid off all our debts and had made an $80,000 profit.

"Other clammers started complaining that we were catching too many clams and the state put in catch limits. At first we were limited to forty bushels a day, the following year the limit was twenty-five, and the year after that it went to fifteen. We kept one boat for each partner and sold off the others. With the limits, we had to buy from other clammers because we couldn't pay to send out all those boats. This worked out well for us because the price went up.

"By now it was about 1960 and Fletcher's business was also suffering. He had to sell off his boats and bought clams from independent clammers like we did. He and I became good friends later on. He'd call me and buy oysters and clams from us when he was short."

Willy's business was called the Tidewater Clam Co. They shucked clams from July 4th until September, and ran two shifts daily. From October until New Year's, they shucked oysters, again in two shifts. From New Year's on, they cut back to one shift. Business was so brisk that they had to buy up to 1,000 bushels of oysters a day for shucking in the plant. There were 150 shuckers working there.

"One day, a DNR representative came into the plant and told me that the state would like to buy all the oyster shells from us (after they had been shucked)," said Willy. "He said the state would pay us two cents a bushel for the shells. I told him we were getting 40 cents a bushel for them now, why should we sell them at a loss. We refused to sell to the state and every year they threatened to take our license. We were selling our shells locally to people who were building houses, etc. They'd use them as a base for their driveways and roads. Some were used for breakwaters, even.

"Processing oysters was a hard business. You had to watch what you were doing. There was a lot of competition and, many times, that competition influenced the market. When oysters were plentiful, the market prices would go down. If they were scarce, prices would be fairly good. A man came in one day and told me that the way to make money in the oyster business was to put extra water in the cans after they'd been shucked. That way, not as many oysters would have to be placed in each can.

"We had a drain in the plant and it ran down into a ditch, which, in turn, emptied into Harris Creek. I had traps in the drain that caught the solids and prevented them from going any further. Small bits and pieces of oysters and clams would flow out of the drain and, at the end of the drain, ten or fifteen snapping turtles hung around there and fed off the drain. There were also muskrats in the area that fed from the drain.

"A federal official came to the plant one day and told me that the water going into the ditch had to be treated. I had to put a chlorinator on the end of the drain. After the chlorinator was installed, there were two pipes coming up from it and I had to put a chlorine tablet in each pipe every day. As the water poured through, it would melt the tablet. Two weeks after I started putting in the chlorine, I went out to the end of the drain and all the animals that had been living there were dead. The chlorine killed them.

"About that time, the state made all the towns put in sewer lines and we noticed changes in the clam population. I used to clam in an area where a development called Rio Vista is located. They ran a pipe out in the river in the area where I clammed. They told us that we couldn't clam in that area any longer. Within two weeks after that pipe went in, there wasn't a clam in the whole Miles River.

"Now they catch razor clams there. These are used for crab bait — humans can't eat them. But there hasn't been a maninose caught there since then. Eventually, white clams disappeared from all other parts of the Bay. Love Point, Rock Hall, the Chester River, Kent Island — I've clammed in all those areas, but there's nothing there now.

"After being in business for thirty years, we could see what was happening to the seafood business. Clams and oysters were not as plentiful and it was not as profitable. We sold the business to the United Shellfish Company in Kent Island. The head man was after me for a couple of years to run the place for him, but I never did. The place never reopened. It is a storage building now. Some of our competitors held on too long and went bankrupt. They lost everything they had; their business, their homes, everything.

"I don't think the Bay'll ever come back like it was. As long as those pipes are out there, the Bay won't be any better. The state won't admit their mistake. They won't admit that they were wrong. The Bay'll never be the same.

"I'll be seventy-nine in July and I don't like the idea of getting old. I want to stay active; I don't like laying around. For the last five or six years, I've been charter fishing. It keeps me busy and brings in a little extra income.

"I like to fish. I kept my boat that I used for clamming, the *Big Will* (I named her for my father), and I use her for charter fishing. I take out fishing parties from April till December and really enjoy it. When some of the other guys in the business go out for a day of fishing, they can't wait to get back in again. That's not me; I'll stay out there

Big Will. Courtesy of Willy Roe, Jr.

Willy and Molly aboard *Big Will*.
Courtesy of Willy Roe, Jr.

so long that the people have to beg me to take them in. I always try to catch my limit. I had a party last year that was three hours late getting here. We went out and, after a while, some of them said they'd like to go in early. I told them that I waited three hours for them to show up, now they had to wait three hours for me to take them in. We stayed till the evening and the fish came up and they caught their limit. They were tickled to death then.

"One of my steady customers is the coach from the Detroit Lions football team. He lives nearby. One time I was in a Ducks Unlimited Tournament and had nineteen rockfish on the lines at the same time. We landed all of them. All of them were over forty inches and weighed between twenty and thirty pounds. One fish was fifty-three inches long and weighed forty-seven pounds. We won the tournament with that fish.

"I used to like to dance a little and drink a little whiskey, but I don't do any of that anymore. I used to like to hunt ducks and play baseball, but I don't do any of that anymore either. I've changed and so has this island. At one time I knew everybody on here, but not anymore. We were like a great big family; we helped each other as often as we were needed. Now, the island is full of strangers and people we don't know. I used to have a dog named Molly. She was a friendly dog and it seemed like everybody on the island knew her. We'd be riding down the road in my truck and people would wave to Molly and call her by name, but I didn't know who those people were. My dog knew more people on the island than I did.

"I love it out there on the water. I'd rather be out there than on land any day. When I go out there, I'm in no hurry to get back in. I was raised out there; I just love this way of life. I hope it never changes for me. I grew up, and still live, in paradise."

CHAPTER SEVEN

Dallas Bradshaw

Once hailed as the Seafood Capital of the World, more oysters were processed in the town of Crisfield, Maryland, than any other town on the eastern seaboard and, possibly, the entire United States. Processing plants lined the spacious waterfront and, from there, shipments were made to cities across the nation and beyond. Crisfield's harbor sheltered an array of vessels devoted to the oyster trade. During the waning years of the nineteenth century, more boats were registered in the town than any other location on the east coast. Some claimed that more boats sailed from Crisfield than any other port in the United States.

Nearby, Tangier Sound was loaded with oysters and the abundance of the bivalve required a tremendous labor force to man the boats and work in the processing plants. A Gold Rush mentality resulted and men flocked to the town, searching for their share of the riches that lay beneath the cool waters surrounding Crisfield.

Crisfield witnessed a prosperity that few Maryland towns shared. The seafood industry brought in a great deal of money and the population grew. By the turn of the twentieth century, Crisfield's population had swollen to 25,000, making it the second largest town in the state. Only Baltimore was larger.

As the years advanced, the ravages of pollution and over-harvesting negatively affected the oyster population in the Chesapeake and Crisfield suffered. Eventually, disease attacked the oyster beds that had been so prolific and all but wiped them out of the Bay. The population of the town dwindled to a few thousand and the economy suffered. In addition to oysters, the waters surrounding Crisfield were loaded with crabs. During the warm season, the abundance of the blue crab provided the financial reward for the citizens of the town. Ultimately, crab processing replaced oyster processing and it remains one of the primary influences on the town's economy. The original town slogan was replaced with a new one, The Crab Capital of the World.

Today, Crisfield and the surrounding area tenaciously cling to a dependency on the Chesapeake. This dependency has created a unique culture and heritage enjoyed by few other locations. Relatively isolated on Maryland's Eastern Shore, many of the people in this geographic area remember a time when fierce independence characterized the citizenry. Customs that are centuries' old are reflected in their lifestyle. Traces of an Elizabethan culture, reflective of their Anglo-Saxon heritage, dominates their speech patterns. These are proud folks who value the closeness of their communities and the principles of our founding fathers. Fairness, caring, faith, and authenticity are a few of the traits that are held in high esteem.

One of Crisfield's more colorful citizens is Dallas Bradshaw. Born in 1927, Bradshaw worked on the waters of the Chesapeake from the time he was a young lad. He was active in both the crabbing and oyster industries before his retirement approximately twenty-five years ago. Dallas was born and raised on isolated Smith Island, Maryland's only remaining inhabited offshore island. Shortly after his birth in the town of Tylerton, his parents moved to a settlement called Long Branch. "My grandfather owned thirteen houses over there," he said. "Long Branch was about a mile from Tylerton. It was nothing but marsh over there and it was connected to Tylerton by a narrow wooden bridge and an oyster-shell path. The people in all the houses were kin to grandfather. Seemed like all the men over to Long Branch owned dredge boats."

When he was five years old, Dallas and his family moved back to Tylerton. "We moved because of convenience," he stated. "The church was at Tylerton and a store was there." Folks who had previously resided in Long Branch gradually began migrating to Tylerton. As the citizens of Long Branch moved, their houses were also relocated to Tylerton. "There was a man named Cox who had a great big scow," Dallas explained. "He'd put rollers under the scow, winch the houses on a board, and then they'd move the scow to wherever the houses would end up. Two boys worked with him; they were really strong — each one of them was as strong as two men. Some of the boys from the community would also help to load the houses on the scow."

Bradshaw was pleased to be returning to Tylerton to live. "All my friends also moved to Tylerton, it was good living there," he stated. "When I was eight or ten years old, my dad had a skiff built for me; it was the greatest thing that ever happened to me. I watched her (the skiff) just like a baby. Grandfather found a couple of poles and he made me a mast and sprit and rigged up a sail that grandmother had made out of feed sacks. Grandmother would wash those sails with lye soap to make them white. She did this every year that I had the boat. There was no rudder, I steered the boat with a paddle.

"Of an evening when the tide was up, a bunch of us boys who had boats would get together and race. The boats would turn over if you weren't careful. We'd carry fifty-pound bags of sand to use as ballast. Sometimes, when we changed tacks, we'd have to move the sandbag to the windward side of the boat. Some of the boats had centerboards, but mine didn't. I had a leeboard hung from the side of the boat. I could change it to the other side if I needed to when I'd come about."

Dallas's boat was about sixteen feet long and the sides were painted white. The interior was painted pea green and the washboards were orange — typical Smith Island workboat colors of the day. The bottom was coated with copper paint to discourage marine growth.

"I hadn't had the boat very long," Dallas laughed. "One day after I come into the dock, I left the sails up. After I went on home, grandfather come down to the dock and took the sail out of my boat and locked it in his outhouse (storage building). He kept it there for three or four days. I didn't leave the sails up anymore after that."

Dallas used his skiff for netting crabs (plucking them off the bottom with his net). His father crab-scraped (using a dredge similar to an oyster dredge, dragging it over the bottom) and would tow Dallas's boat to the crabbing grounds. "We'd crab over to Jenkins Creek," Dallas continued. "I'd net a bushel or two every day. When I thought I'd caught enough, I'd tell dad I was going to sail on home. He'd watch for me to make sure I didn't get into any trouble."

The focus of his crabbing was to catch peelers. "Most of the time they'd be attached to male crabs (while involved in the mating process)," he said. "We called them doublers." To separate the crabs, Dallas would toss the crabs into the air, forcing the pair to disengage. He would re-catch the female (peeler) in his net as it fell through the air while the male crab returned to the water. "That Jimmy (male crab) would go down and find him another wife in an hour," Dallas chuckled.

The peeler would be placed in a "live box" built into the bottom of the boat. The live box sat atop holes that were bored through the bottom of the boat to allow water to flow inside. Peelers would eventually shed their shells and become soft crabs. Thereafter, they were shipped to far-off places in wooden crates filled with sea grass to keep them alive during the journey. "There wasn't much market for hard crabs in those days," said Bradshaw. "Once in a great while we could sell a few though. We'd send them to New York for the market there. Only soft crabs brought any money back then.

"My dad taught me how to swim the Smith Island way. He tied a piece of rope around my waist and we walked out on the pier; then he told me to jump overboard. He said that I should do whatever I had to do to stay on top of the water — kick my feet, paddle my hands. After two or three times up and down the wharf, I could swim. That's how all the boys on the island learned to swim. Later on I swam so much that dad said he was going to have to paint my bottom with copper paint."

Weather was always a factor for those living on Smith Island. "It seemed like it would freeze up bad every year," stated Dallas. He said that 1936 was a real bad year for ice. "It snowed every night and the Bay and Tangier Sound were frozen solid. Every night a plane would fly in to Tylerton to bring supplies. A bunch of people walked across the ice from Smith Island to Crisfield…that's how thick the ice was.

"One winter, when I was twelve years old, there was a lot of ice in the Bay. It was frozen all the way across. Ice was so thick that the skipjacks from the island couldn't get home for Christmas like they usually did. My dad was on one of the skipjack crews and they were stuck over to the Potomac. After a while, they were able to get off the boats and come home on a bus. When they got to Crisfield, they got on the mail boat, *Island Belle*, and headed toward Smith Island. The *Island Belle* was able to break the ice and get right close to Tylerton before she got bogged down in the thicker ice. The skipjack crews walked across the ice to get home. The next morning, my dad and I went back to the *Island Belle* in my grandfather's sleigh to help unload her. My dad told me to climb up on top of the pilothouse to get a sack of potatoes. 'There's something else up there too,' he said. When I climbed up to the top of the cabin, there was a bike up there. I never had a bike before. It was a second-hand bike and dad had paid $5 for it. That was a lot of money back then. Boy, was I happy! I laid that sack of potatoes across the basket and peddled that bike right across the ice to Tylerton. Come right straight down the channel, clean into town like that."

Dallas related a story about Clinton Corbin, a relative who attended Goldy Beacon College in Wilmington. "Clinton come home from college and got caught in a big freeze up," he said. "He wanted to get back to Wilmington because he had some important examinations to study for. Folks tried to talk him into staying, but Clinton wouldn't have none of that. He was determined to get back to Wilmington. His dad hired a couple of boys, stronger than steel they were. They nailed runners on the bottom of a gunning skiff so she would go across the ice.

"They put Clinton in that skiff and headed across to Crisfield. The going was rough and it took a long time. Along the way, a goose dropped from out of the sky; it had a broken wing. They threw the goose in the boat and kept on going. By the time they reached Ole Island, the sun was a going down and it was snowing so thick that they could barely see where they were headed. Somehow, they made it into Crisfield and met up with the town doctor. The doctor saw that goose and told them that if they'd give him the goose he'd buy them dinner. 'All you can eat,' he told them. They handed over the goose and they had their dinner, just like the doctor had said."

Dallas attended the local school in Tylerton for the elementary years. His mother insisted that he continue to high school, so the family rented a house in Crisfield during the school year and Dallas attended Crisfield High School. "I really didn't like school very much," he said. "I did enjoy playing sports though. My cousin, Waverly Evans, and I went to high school together. He was one of the fastest runners anywhere. One day, Puckers Parks, who was a member of the track team, asked us if there was anybody on Smith Island that could run. I told him that Wave could beat anybody over here. 'You're kidding,' said Puckers. 'Try him,' I told him. Puckers got him to run and he just flew. Puckers put Waverly on the track team and he ran the final leg of the relay. He was really something.

"One day, years later, my son and I were walking along with Waverly over on Tylerton. Waverly was in his late 60s or 70s by that time. I was telling my son about how fast Waverly could run when he was younger. My son looked at Waverly and said, 'Dad says you can run.' Waverly pulled off his cap, looked at my son, and said, 'You want to race?' My son got so tickled he bent over double just a laughing."

When school was out for the year, Dallas and his family would return to their home on Smith Island. "I only went to the tenth grade," he said. "Dad needed me to help him. Times were tough back then."

When Dallas was a teenager, he was a member of the crew on a skipjack. "The skipjack was named *Wilma Florence* and my uncle, Eddie Evans, was the captain," said Bradshaw. "Every evening after supper the five of us on the crew would sit in the cabin and listen to my uncle tell yarns. He was real good at telling yarns. One night he said that when you meet another boat coming toward you and you waver (wave) to the crew in the other boat, they'll return the waver in the same way. 'No way,' I thought then. One day we were dredging on Seven Foot Knoll near the Patapsco River outside of Baltimore and I was steering. I looked up and here come a boat toward us. I said, 'Boys, here's where we check out Uncle Ed's yarn. We'll see what he does.' The rest of the crew stopped working and just watched. When the boat got off against us, I wavered. I bent down and threw my hand around in a strange way. Don't you know that the man on the other boat wavered back in exactly the same way? I guess Uncle Ed was right after all."

Crewing on the skipjack was not always pleasant. "We stayed on the boat for five months during the coldest part of the year," said Dallas. "We'd sleep on it and live on it during the time we were away. When we worked near Baltimore, we'd rent a room on weekends. It cost us $5 for a weekend. We used the room to take showers.

"We'd miss home while we were away on the dredge boat. I remember one time we were sailing home just before Christmas. When the lights of Smith Island come into view, I thought that was the prettiest sight I'd ever seen. Smith Island really looked good."

Eventually, Dallas would work on other skipjacks in addition to the *Wilma Florence*. One of the boats he crewed on was the *Ruby Ford*. Built in Somerset County in 1891, the *Ford* had the reputation of being a very seaworthy boat. "She was really able," said Dallas. "She could handle a lot of wind. She was good in a breeze and fast, too."

In 1945, Dallas enlisted in the Navy. "I was only seventeen and my dad had to sign for me to go," laughed the jovial Bradshaw. "I stayed in the Navy for three years, three months, and three days. After finishing boot camp, I was sent to Camp Peary on the York River in Virginia for further training. That was the muddiest place I ever did see. We went down there and pulled alongside an AKA (amphibious ship). The AKA carried twenty-four boats on her, 56-foot LCM's (landing craft), and others.

"They were handing out jobs one day and a wise guy looked at me and asked, 'What can you do?' I told him I could run any of those boats. 'Give me fifteen or twenty minutes to get used her and I can put her anywhere,' I told him. He laughed and yelled, 'Hey chief, we got us a captain here.' The chief said, 'You say you can run one of them LCMs?' I told him to give me fifteen or twenty minutes in her to see what she can do. 'All right, you're going to get your fifteen or twenty minutes,' he said. They gave me a bow man and a stern man and put me into the boat. She had twin 671 diesel engines and I told the men, 'I want you to hold on — stay in this boat, 'cause if you fall overboard I might run over you.' After I ran her a few minutes, the chief yelled, 'Bring her in here (to the dock) captain!' I threw the throttles open and come in toward the dock with a lot of headway. As I got closer, the men standing on the dock started to move backwards. When I got near the dock, I backed her down and spun her around to lay side to the pier. She stopped right still without hitting a thing. The chief looked down and said, 'Well, I'll be damned if we don't have us a coxswain.'

"After that, they made me a seaman first class and I ran the boats. One time we were underway from Norfolk in the AKA bound for New York. One of the boys on the boat come down with appendicitis. The doctor was away from our ship and the Captain asked if I thought I could carry the man over to a cruiser that was about two miles away where there was a surgeon. It was thick foggy. I told the captain to give me the range and the bearing and I could get him there. I got the man there without much trouble. That cruiser come right up out of the fog and it seemed like it was bigger than the world. The officer on deck told me he thought I should stay on the cruiser until the fog lifted. I told him I'd like to return to my ship in spite of the fog. I didn't realize it, but the captain was looking down on us and he yelled down to the officer, 'Let him go.' We got underway and after while something appeared out of the fog. One of the men on my boat asked me what it was. 'If it ain't our ship, it must be an island,' I told him.

"Later, we took training down to Mobile, Alabama. One day I had everyone on board my boat, except the engineer. In a little while, a new man got on board and asked if I was Coxswain Bradshaw. 'Yes, that I am,' I said. We talked and I asked him where he was from. He said, 'You'll never know. I come from a way-back place. Did you ever hear of Crisfield, Maryland?' I said, 'Yeah, I've heard of it. You ever hear of a place called Smith Island? That's where I'm from.' He was so glad to see me that he hugged me. We became good friends after that."

Eventually, Dallas served in the Pacific in the San Blas Islands. "One day the LCM I was driving was loaded with 150 barrels of gasoline," said Dallas. "The gasoline was loaded onto two sleighs. I come into the beach and lowered the ramp [in the front of the boat]. The beach officer, from the Army, come down and said, 'Hey coxswain, did you ever unload on a beach like this before?' I answered, 'No sir.' He left and after while he come back with the biggest bulldozer I've ever seen in my life. He said to me, 'I'm going to hook up to one of them sleighs and when I do I want you to open your throttles wide open backwards. If you don't, I'll take your boat and all right up on the beach.' I said to myself, 'This I've got to see.' Well, he hooked onto the sleigh and I had to give her every bit of throttle I had to keep her off the beach. After he got the drums off, he come back down the beach just a-laughing. 'You didn't think I could do that, did you?' I had to admit that I didn't.

"Another time we were just sitting around on our ship and I looked up and here come a bunch of natives paddling a 30-foot boat. The boat was loaded down with bananas. They pulled alongside our ship and asked if we wanted to buy some. We bought every one of them bananas. They were the biggest bananas I'd ever seen. Boy, were they good. You could smell those bananas all over the ship. They really smelled good.

"One time I come home on leave and went over to see my grandmother. People on Smith Island collected rainwater from their roofs and it ran down into cisterns. During my visit, grandmother sent me over to a neighbor's house with a pitcher to get some rainwater from their cistern. My grandmother always claimed that rainwater made the best coffee. 'I'll give you a quarter if you go,' she told me. I told her I didn't want nothing for doing that and went over and filled the pitcher. When I got back, she wasn't around, so I set the pitcher on the table and left. I didn't see her again for eighteen months. When I come home again, I went to see her. After giving me a big hug, she put a quarter in my hand."

After being discharged from the Navy, Dallas returned to Smith Island. He bought a 29-foot crab scrape boat. Once on the boat, the peelers that have been caught are separated from the SAV, taken to crab shanties, and placed in tanks, where they are allowed to shed their shells and become soft crabs.

"My scraping boat had been rigged by Captain Johnny Tyler," Bradshaw explained. "She had a beam (width) of seven or eight feet. She had a CB radio and she had a centerboard in her from the days when she was a sailboat. I got a good buy on that boat. I paid $450 for her and she had a 25-horsepower, Universal marine engine in her. There must've been twenty-five boats in Tylerton that had Universal motors in them in those days. The boats all sounded alike when they were running. I had a dog in those days, his name was Bingo. When I left the dock of a morning in my boat, Bingo would lay on the wharf and wait for me to come home. When the boats come home after working all day, they'd pass by the wharf and old Bingo wouldn't pay them no mind. He'd just lay there real calm-like. But when I come in the creek he'd get all excited and dance around. I don't understand how he could tell the sound of my boat from the others with the same engine. That dog was really something."

No stranger to unlawful activities, Dallas was arrested a few times for illegally catching oysters. "We'd go over to the Potomac River of a night and power-dredge for oysters," said Dallas. "Except in Somerset County, power-dredging was illegal in the state of Maryland. One night there were thirteen of us over there from Smith Island. We were dredging and here come the law on us. The marine police had a rifle on board and they fired on us. My boat never got hit, but others did. They shined bright lights on us and arrested us on the spot. When I saw them coming, I cut the line that ran to the dredge and threw over the oysters I had caught. Even though I didn't have no oysters, they arrested me anyway. Just because I was there!

"They threw us in jail over to Leonardtown and I had a chance to make a phone call. I called a fellow back home who was into politics and told him I was in jail with a bunch of other Smith Islanders. 'What the hell are you doing in jail?' he said. Then he asked who the state's attorney was over there. I told him and he said, 'I went to college with that man. I'll have you out in ten minutes.' Sure enough, we were all free within ten minutes. One of the guys, though, told the officers that he didn't want to leave the jail right then. He wanted to wait till the next morning so he could get his free breakfast."

Following World War II, islanders formed a baseball team and played teams from around the Bay area. Among other places, games were held against teams from Cambridge, Rock Hall, Deal Island, Crisfield, mainland Virginia, and Tangier Island. Dallas was a member of the team. "We'd play a game every Saturday," Dallas explained. "We were really pretty good, one year our record was 22-2. If we played at home, and if the team we were playing was from the mainland, we'd have to meet them and take them over to Smith Island in our boats. When we got there, we'd feed them real good before we played the game. Lots of times they'd be so full of Smith Island ten-layered cake that they couldn't play as well as they ordinarily would have.

"One time we played over to Reedville, Virginia. There was a retired Pittsburg Pirates pitcher named Joe Muir who lived just outside of Salisbury. Some of the boys knew him and we took him with us to Reedville. Reedville had a really good team. Waverly Evans was the first man at bat. He hit a homerun. Boy, he really tagged that thing. The ball went over the road and into a field. When it come our turn to take the field, we put Joe Muir on the mound. He threw so fast that you couldn't even see the ball. We beat them so bad that they quit on us in the seventh inning. They couldn't hit Joe. We went 7-0 against them that ycar.

"I batted against Joe one time during practice. I got a hit the first time I took the bat. 'Bet you can't do that again,' he told me. The next time I took the bat, he threw a change-up. That ball was in the catcher's mitt while I was still swinging. He was some pitcher.

"This one Saturday we played over to Tangier Island. That's when I met Kakie (Catherine, who would later become his wife). She couldn't take her eyes off of me that day. She fell hard for me while I was playing ball.

"On weekends, four or five of us would go over to Tangier Island and go a-courting. We'd rent a room for the weekend and stay overnight. I courted Kakie for about a year that way before we were married. We got married on Smith Island in 1949 and went

Dallas and Kakie Bradshaw.
Courtesy of Edward R. Theiler III.

to Baltimore for our honeymoon. We spent two or three days up there. We went to the Hippodrome Theater and watched a show that a singer named Don Cornell was in."

Musically inclined, Kakie sang and played the guitar with the Smith Island Ladies Quartet for twenty-two years. They traveled extensively and made records. "They went down to South Carolina to make their records," said Dallas. "She also sang to a lot of funerals. We counted up that she sang at over 450 funerals. We've been married now for sixty-four years. My pet name for her is 'gorgeous hunk of femininity'."

Three sons resulted from the union. "Mark and Jim are both in their fifties now," Dallas said. "They both work over to Princess Anne at the prison. They worked on the water with me for a while, but when the prison opened they went there. When they worked with me, we worked out of a boat I named *Mark and Jim*. She was a 36-foot deadrise and was built in 1967. Our youngest son, Jon, drowned when he was eighteen years old. He had graduated from high school just ten days before he died. He was in an outboard boat one night and the boat had no running lights. Another boat was out there with no running lights and they collided with one another. I've never been the same since. That's the reason we moved to Crisfield. Every day I had to pass the spot where he was drowned. That really worked on me. That was twenty-five or thirty years ago."

Following his move to Crisfield, Dallas began working with the Chesapeake Bay Foundation (CBF). He became the Captain of the Foundation's boat, *Aunt Allie II*. He also managed the lodge at the CBF outpost on Great Fox Island, just over the state line in Virginia waters, and became a much sought-after raconteur of ghost stories and other tales. Public and private school students, along with their teachers and parents, came to the outpost for three-day periods during the warm season. By taking the students out on *Aunt Alley II*, Dallas familiarized them with the ways of the Chesapeake. "I'd show them how to crab scrape, tong for oysters, and fish," he said. "There'd be twenty students at a time and I'd have two different groups every week."

Students would stay in a lodge that dated to 1929. When it was built, it was a privately-owned hunting and fishing lodge. Eventually, it was donated to the CBF. In addition to his duties on *Aunt Alley II*, Dallas also served as an environmental educator. When students were on the island, he stayed in the lodge along with the other chaperones. "We really had very little trouble with the students," he stated. "One time, though, a boy got a little restless and started misbehaving. I went to him and told him that if he didn't soon straighten up I was going to put him in my boat and take him back to Crisfield. I told him that he would be on his own then to fend for himself and get back home any way he could. He calmed right down and we didn't have any more problems with him while he was there.

"The first thing I'd do when a new group of kids come to the island was to fix them a good dinner. I had some crab pots set out and I'd catch and steam up a bunch of big Jimmies. We'd also have soft crabs, fried fish, and oysters.

"A group of kids from Norfolk come one time and their teacher was one of the chaperones. I asked if she'd ever ate an oyster. She said that she never had. 'You're from Norfolk and you ain't never ate an oyster?' I asked her. She said she'd try it. I fried up seven oysters and put them between two slices of bread and handed it to her. I told her that if she didn't eat it, I would. She looked at it for a minute and took a bite. Then she looked at me and said, 'You'll not get this sandwich back,' and kept right on eating til it was gone." Dallas worked with CBF for about ten years, until his retirement in the 1990s.

In spite of the fact that he has lived in Crisfield for a great many years, at heart he still considers himself a Smith Islander rather than a Crisfielder. He has fond memories of living on Smith Island and his days working the Chesapeake. "It's all I know," the affable Bradshaw said. "It's been a good life."

CHAPTER EIGHT

Floyd F. Azbell, Jr.

Since the early 1800s, there has been a lighthouse in the Atlantic Ocean marking the path for ships as they travel into the Chesapeake Bay. Known as the Chesapeake Light, initially the light was mounted on anchored ships known as lightships, lightboats, or lightvessels. The *Chesapeake Lightship* was the first to be placed into service in U. S. waters.

Lightships initially were anchored sailing vessels. Later, steam-powered vessels were utilized. The first lightship in the Chesapeake was stationed off Willoughby Spit near Norfolk. Known simply as No. 46, the ship was of steel construction sheathed with wood. The vessel was designed to withstand harsh weather conditions and hosted a crew of four who were on duty for four months at a time.

More recently, lightships were of steel construction, specifically designed for the tasks they were to endure. Lightships were not named; instead, they were assigned a number. The name of the station where the ship was assigned was written on the sides of the hull in large bold letters, however; thus enabling entering ships to know with certainty the body of water they were nearing. By 1983, over one hundred lightship stations had been established on the waters of the U. S.

Arguably, the best-known lightship to serve the Chesapeake Bay was LV-116. Stationed 14.5 miles from the Virginia mainland, at the mid-point between Cape Charles and Cape Henry, the ship began her career guarding the Chesapeake in 1933.

Built in 1930 in Charleston, South Carolina at a cost of $274,000, the LV-116 was 133 feet in length with a thirty-foot beam and a fifteen-foot draft. The 130-ton vessel was held on station by a 5,000-pound anchor attached to 1,000 feet of heavy chain. She was propelled by a 350-horsepower diesel engine, which gave the ship a top speed of nine knots. The light atop one of her two masts, used to warn ships entering the Bay, was visible for twenty-four miles and generated 13,000 candle power.

A complement of sixteen men was assigned to the lightship; ten seamen, five officers, and a cook comprised the staff. Primarily, their duties revolved around maintaining the light as an aid to navigation. They worked in shifts; two weeks on and two weeks off. Crewmembers slept in rooms with double bunks, officers in single rooms. Two separate dining rooms — one for officers, the other for lower-ranked crew — were adjacent to the living quarters. The Captain enjoyed a private stateroom near the pilothouse.

Pressed into military service during World War II, the familiar red-hulled vessel was repainted battleship grey and removed from her station. She was assigned a post in Massachusetts as an examination vessel. After the war, her red paint was restored and she was returned to her original station off Virginia's coast.

Storms were an expected occurrence for members of the crew. In 1933, 1936, and again in 1962, heavy seas and rough weather caused the main anchor chain to snap and the ship had to use its engine to remain on station while a secondary anchor was dropped. During the storm of 1962, a gigantic wave broke over the ship's twenty-foot-high bow and severely damaged her pilothouse, carrying away much of the equipment previously attached to her deck. The vessel got underway and headed for the Coast Guard station in Portsmouth, Virginia. Repairs were made very quickly and the lightship returned to her station within twenty-four hours.

In 1965, after serving the shipping industry for over thirty years, the LV-116 departed from the Chesapeake station. Her last day on station was September 25th. Replacing the lightship was a permanent light platform. The LV-116 circled the platform several times before heading to the Coast Guard station in Portsmouth, Virginia.

The LV-116 finished her career at the entrance to Delaware Bay. She served on that location until 1970. Now on display in Baltimore, the ship is restored and open to the public. The vessel is listed as a National Historic Landmark. Once again, the word "Chesapeake" is proudly emblazoned on her sides.

Erected at a cost of $1.7 million, the light station that replaced LV-116 resembles the Texas Tower oil rigs in the Gulf of Mexico. The station was staffed by members of the United States Coast Guard. Floyd F. Azbell, Jr. served on the Chesapeake Light Station during his early years as a member of the Coast Guard.

"I always wanted to be a lighthouse keeper," he said. "My vision of a keeper was a bearded man in a yellow slicker, with a pipe in his mouth and a lantern in his hand. I found out that modern-day lighthouse keepers are a whole lot different."

Floyd (Butch) Azbell joined the Coast Guard after graduating from Stephen Decatur High School near Ocean City, Maryland. "I had wanted to join the Air Force because my dad had retired from the Air Force," Butch said. "But when I got to the recruiting office, I noticed a mural of a 44-foot Coast Guard cutter breaking through the surf and it looked exciting. I started talking to the Coast Guard recruiter and soon forgot about the Air Force. The recruiter said the Coast Guard would be happy to take me. I agreed and was signed up on the spot and was scheduled to leave the following October.

"I told them I'd like to be involved in aviation electronics. Later, after taking a test, I discovered I was color blind and that limited my career field choice. I knew a little about plumbing because I'd studied it during high school and was working a summer job doing plumbing for a swimming pool company. They said I could become involved with damage control. Damage control people, they explained, were the folks who fixed things, welded, did plumbing and carpentry. I agreed and continued working for the pool company that summer.

"I was working at Bethany Beach, Delaware, at the Sea Colony resort, installing a pool and it was very hot. The Coast Guard called and asked if I could report earlier. They wanted me to go in August. I was tired of the heat, so I agreed to go early.

"I was only seventeen at the time, so my mother had to sign for me in order to enlist. She didn't want to do it; she had never cared for the military lifestyle. She wanted me to do better. I told her that if she didn't sign, I'd go in October anyway when I reached eighteen. Reluctantly, she gave her permission and I was off to Boot Camp that summer. It turned out that joining the Coast Guard was the best thing I ever did."

Finishing Boot Camp, Azbell was sent to Miami Beach, Florida, for an assignment aboard the *USCGC* (United States Coast Guard Cutter) *Hollyhock*, a 180-foot buoy tender. "I had told them that I didn't want to go to a school," he said. "I didn't like school and didn't want to attend one in the Coast Guard. On the *Hollyhock*, I worked in the engine room for thirty days and then scrubbed pots and pans for thirty days; then I would repeat the cycle. The work wasn't to my liking. I began to regret that I hadn't gone to school. At the time, there was a one-and-a-half-year waiting period to get into damage control school, but they said I could get into machinery technician school in six months. Within two months, I was in machinery tech school in Yorktown, Virginia. The training was sixteen weeks in duration. Machinery technicians dealt with everything mechanical on a ship; generators, fire pumps, and propulsion engines were all the domain of machinery technicians. I requested to be sent to a lightstation after completing machine tech school.

"Many lightstations were either on shore or close to shore. That was my idea of lightstation duty. When I found out that I was being sent to the Chesapeake Light Station, I was a little leery. Cheslight was considered a semi-isolated duty station and I was concerned about being stuck fourteen miles offshore with a bunch of guys."

Butch was promoted to 3rd class (E-4) and reported to Cheslight in February 1977. Supported by four 33-inch, concrete-filled, steel pilings driven 180 feet into the ocean floor, the station was located in seventy feet of water. Standing eighty feet above the surface of the ocean, the station had the word "Chesapeake" written on each of its sides. Comprised of three levels, the station was forty feet square. The roof served as the helicopter landing deck. A 37-foot tower was located on that level, which housed the light. At night, the light was visible for twenty-four miles. Living quarters were located on the middle level. There were six single bedrooms for crewmembers. In addition to the bedrooms, the radio room, recreation room, and galley were on the middle deck. The bottom deck was the maintenance deck, where generators, the heating system, and fire-control equipment were located.

"Six men were assigned to the station," Butch explained. "An electrician, electrical technician, fireman, officer in charge, engineer, and machinery technician made up the staff. Four men were on station at all times and two were off. We worked twenty-eight days straight and then had fourteen days off. The tour of duty on Cheslight was eighteen months.

"We did our own cooking and, for the most part, we ate very well. Each of us took turns cooking. The electrician on the station, though, was from Bluefield, West Virginia, and he couldn't cook at all. Once, when he cooked breakfast, he failed to put any grease in the frying pan before trying to cook eggs. The pan was burned so badly that we had to throw it away. The Officer in Charge had each of us cook dinner for one week. We had some good meals. We were allowed two beers a day while on station. When on ships, we were allowed two beers on morale night also."

During Azbell's fourteen days off station, he would return home to the Ocean City area. The youngest of three boys, Butch was born in Cambridge, England, in 1957 while his father was stationed there. "When I was two years old, dad was transferred to Andrews Air Force Base near Washington, D.C.," said Butch. "Following his retirement, dad got a job with a vending company and they had the very first contract for the concession on Assateague Island. We'd live there in the summers while my parents managed the snack bar concession on Assateague beach.

Chesapeake Light Station. *Courtesy of Floyd Azbell, Jr.*

"When I was nine, my parents divorced. My mother and I moved into a little bungalow behind an egg hatchery and I attended Snow Hill Elementary School in Worcester County. Eventually, we moved to Berlin and I attended schools there, graduating in 1975 from Stephan Decatur High. I also attended Worcester Vocational School for a portion of each day and learned plumbing, the career I followed until I entered the Coast Guard."

Following his fourteen-day leave in Ocean City, Butch would return to the Coast Guard Station in Portsmouth, Virginia. "The night before we were to return to the lightstation, we had to sleep in a barracks in Portsmouth," he said. "The crew that was on duty at the station would radio a shopping list for us and we would go to the commissary the next day and fill the order. We'd buy toiletries, food, cigarettes, etc. for the next month. We'd also bring any supplies and spare parts that were needed, and then we'd take the order either to an 82-foot patrol boat or a helicopter for the trip to the station. If we went by patrol boat, it was a two-hour trip, but if we were lucky enough to go on a helicopter, the trip was only fifteen minutes. Those trips carrying supplies were called log runs."

Drinking water was delivered to the station by a buoy tender. The buoy tender also brought diesel fuel for the generators and the heating boiler. Rain water was collected from the helo deck and supplemented the supply of drinking water. "When it started raining, we'd wait thirty minutes or so for the rain to wash off the bird droppings, etc., then we'd shut a valve, and collect the water," Butch explained. "The rain would go into the drinking water tank."

Light tower on Chesapeake Light Station.
Courtesy of Floyd Azbell, Jr.

If the crew wanted a suntan, they went up to the light tower. "It was sweltering hot up there," Butch laughed. "The glass in the tower just collected the heat and it was so hot that we called it our sauna."

The crew ran out of cigarettes once while Butch was stationed on the light. "We had life rafts on the station that were left over from World War II," he explained. "In each raft were emergency supplies. We were told that cigarettes were included in the supplies. We broke into some of the rations, but there were no cigarettes. There was some chocolate candy though. We really enjoyed eating that."

Butch stated that when he initially reported to the station, he went through an initiation ritual. "They put me on the midnight to 8 a.m. watch," he said. "They had explained beforehand that the lightstation was haunted. I was told that one of the workers who had helped build the station was killed while working on it and often visited the light. I was on watch and everybody else was asleep, or so I thought. All of a sudden the rocking chairs in the rec room began to rock by themselves. Within five minutes, all the books on the bookshelf fell off. They had attached fishing lines to the chairs and books and manipulated them after I went on duty. I was a little taken back when all that happened."

There were some moments that made the crew legitimately uneasy, however. "Storms were always unnerving," said Butch. "Storms out there were violent. Winds blew so hard that mirrors on the walls would rattle and shake. Exterior walls were substantial, but interior walls were paper thin. Sometimes, waves were fifteen to twenty feet in height. During storms we weren't allowed to go outside alone. There had to be someone with you. If we had to go down to the maintenance deck to take water temperature (which we did every four hours) or something, walking on the steel mesh deck with the water and waves eighty feet below was scary. In time, we became used to walking on the mesh deck. I guess one of the worst things about storms was the fact that we were trapped on the station. If it was our turn to go ashore, for example, that had to be delayed until the weather cleared."

Because the station was over three miles offshore, sewage was discharged directly into the ocean. "When it was very cold, the sewage pipe would freeze and we couldn't use the head," Butch laughed. "When that happened, we had to use the bucket-and-chuck-it method."

Below the maintenance deck was a lower landing where boats docked. This was only twenty feet above the water. From the lower landing, the crew often fished on off-duty time. "We caught a lot of fish out there," said Butch. "We caught lots of sea bass and amberjacks. Some of those amberjacks weighed forty or fifty pounds. We'd often see big schools of fish circling around the station. Some of those fish were huge also." Crewmembers also swam from the lower landing. A ladder was attached that went down into the water and the cool ocean provided a welcome relief from summer heat.

"We weren't allowed to have CB radios out there," said Butch. "But we snuck one onto the station anyway. Our handle was 'fish haven base'. Fishermen from Virginia Beach would call us for the weather, etc. and they really appreciated that we were there. They'd bring us fast-food from the mainland and cigarettes, etc."

Except for storms, life on the Chesapeake Light Station was fairly uneventful, according to Butch. Days were routine, for the most part. "One time, though, there was a charter boat that came out and tied up to our station," he said. "It was illegal to do that, but we turned a blind-eye this time. The boat was loaded with near naked women. They didn't know the station was manned. We enjoyed watching them fish and sun themselves. After a while, they went on their way and we had had our thrill for the day.

"My bedroom was next to the radio room. A radio beacon signal would go out every few seconds from the radio room. It was morse code to let approaching ships know they were nearing our station. When the signal went out, I could hear it in my bedroom. Also, if it was foggy, a horn would sound every few seconds to warn ships that our station was there. Another sound that inhibited our sleep was the generator. Every time the light would go on, it would pull extra power from the generator and it would surge, so between the generator, the fog horn, and the radio beacon, it was loud. Eventually, we became accustomed to the noise and were able to sleep through it all.

"Big ships would zero in on our radio beacon. Often, they'd be on auto pilot and it was unnerving to see a big ship headed directly toward our station at thirty knots. Even if they were a couple of miles away, they looked like they were on top of us; they were so huge. When we saw one coming, we'd call it on the radio and ask their intentions. After we called, we'd see them swerve a little and head toward the entrance to the Bay. Lots of times, I'm sure, the man on watch was probably asleep."

Butch fell asleep one time while on watch. It was late at night and the TV had gone off the air and the buzzing of the set woke him. "I hadn't been asleep for more than thirty minutes or so," he said. "The radio was calling for the weather conditions. I had slept through my time period for reporting those to the base on the mainland. Also, a sailboat race was scheduled to start that was going from Newport News, Virginia, to Newport, Rhode Island, and they had told me to go out on deck with a searchlight and report the sail numbers of the boats as they went by. I was really concerned because I was afraid they'd already gone by while I was sleeping. The guy on the other end of the radio asked where I had been. I told him I had been out on deck looking for the sailboats and hadn't seen any of them. That's why, I explained, I was late reporting to the base. I made up the weather and sea conditions and passed those on. That was the only time I fell asleep while on duty and it scared me. I'd have been in big trouble if they had caught me. As it turned out, the sailboats didn't go by until almost dawn."

The views from the lightstation were breathtaking. On a clear night, the lights of the Chesapeake Bay Bridge Tunnel could be seen, as well as the ferris wheel at Virginia Beach. During Azbell's tenure on the lightstation, the Commandant of the Coast Guard paid a visit. "He came by helicopter and we laid out quite a spread for lunch," said Butch. "He only stayed a little while; he toured the station and told us we were doing a good job. Then he was gone."

The Chesapeake Light Station was one of the most remote lightstations in the Coast Guard system. In 1980, shortly after Butch's tour ended, the light was automated. Although the station remains, no crew permanently man it. Hurricane Isabel damaged the boat dock and it is no longer used. The station is now only accessible by helicopter.

"I thoroughly enjoyed my time on Cheslight," said Butch. "Serving on the Cheslight was one of the best duty stations I ever had during my entire Coast Guard career."

Since 1997, Cheslight has also become a platform that is used for meteorological research by NASA. In 2004, the Coast Guard conducted a rigid inspection of the station with the thought of dismantling it. The station was declared sound and it remained in use. As a result, Cheslight is the sole remaining Texas Tower station still active.

Following his tour on Cheslight, Butch was assigned to the Ocean City Coast Guard Station. "I was stationed there until 1979 and I was promoted to 2nd class (E-5) while at Ocean City," he said. "My job was dispatching and caring for the small boats assigned to the station. We had a 44-foot cutter, a 41-foot cutter, a 25-foot surf boat, and a 21-footer. I also stood watch in the radio room and sent messages via teletype machine.

"The *Patty B.* was a fishing vessel that went aground on the north jetty. The surf boat went out to tow the boat off the jetty and the weight of the fishing boat rolled the surf boat over. The surf boat righted itself after a few minutes. A friend of mine was on it at the time and his footprints were on the cabin ceiling. A bigger boat was dispatched and towed the fishing vessel in without damage.

"The most memorable rescue that I was personally involved with was a disabled boat just outside the inlet. We had sent a boat out there to help and they radioed back that they needed another pump. Another guy and I got in the 25-foot surf boat and headed toward them. The seas were so bad that we couldn't even get out of the inlet. I was really worried that I might not make it back in to shore. The pump had been tied down and the waves knocked it overboard. It was stored in half of a 55-gallon drum when it went over the side. The crew on the larger boat ended up not needing the other pump after all. Two weeks later, the pump washed ashore at Bethany Beach. We dispatched a truck to go and retrieve it."

One of the strangest rescues Floyd was involved with was a runaway boat. "We got a call that a boat was running in circles on Assawoman Bay," he said. "It had thrown out the driver and kept circling itself. We jumped in the 21-footer and zoomed up the Bay. The boat was going around in circles just as fast as it could. The driver had been rescued by another boat that was on the scene. We went over and put him on our boat. Then we made several unsuccessful attempts to board the speeding boat. We tried to pull alongside the boat for me to jump aboard, but the boat was skidding so much that we couldn't do that. We threw lines out in the water, trying to foul the boat's propeller. That didn't work either. Meanwhile, the boat was getting closer to a buoy each time it came around. The owner was worried that it might strike the buoy and be ruined. Finally, the engine just stopped. We towed the boat back to its slip and conducted an inspection. We gave the owner a citation because the fuel tanks were chained down. In the process of writing the citation, I found that I'd gone to high school with the man. When I see him today, he still reminds me of the citation I wrote."

During the days when Butch was stationed at Ocean City, gasoline prices had increased dramatically. "We found that commercial fishermen would go out to the fishing grounds (100 miles from the mainland), fish, and then run out of fuel," said Floyd. "They planned it that way. They'd only take as much fuel as they needed to get out there and fish, and then they'd call the Coast Guard to tow them home. This was during the fuel crisis when diesel fuel was so costly. This was probably a contributing factor to the manner in which today's Coast Guard rescues vessels. They won't help unless there is imminent danger.

"Another time we rescued a scallop vessel. After we got the boat into port, the crew wanted to know if they could pay us. We refused because that was against regulations. We pulled away and headed for the Coast Guard station and noticed a fishy smell at the back of our boat. The crew had placed a thirty-pound bag of scallops on our boat without our knowledge. We ate scallops broiled, steamed, fried, and baked. They were sure tasty."

After four years of service in the Coast Guard, Butch was discharged and returned home. "After being out for eighty days, I decided to reenlist," said Butch. "When I went back in, I told them I wanted to have shore duty either as a recruiter or instructor." Butch was assigned to Yorktown, Virginia, where he taught in the same school he had attended a few years before. "Some of the old-timers who were instructing at the school felt that I shouldn't have been assigned there," said Floyd. "They didn't feel I had enough experience and hadn't been in long enough to warrant such an assignment."

After being at Yorktown for one year, Butch was promoted to E6. This infuriated the senior staff at the school since it had taken many of them fifteen or more years to gain the rank that Butch had obtained in five years. "I joined at the right time," he said. "A lot of the guys who had been in during Vietnam were getting out and there were shortages in almost all career fields. This was good for me and allowed me to get promotions much faster than normal."

Butch also worked diligently at his job. He enhanced the curriculum by providing hand-outs and diagrams so that the students better understood. In spite of these efforts,

US Coast Guard Cutter *Campbell*.
Courtesy of Floyd Azbell, Jr.

his evaluation reflected below-average performance. "I was appalled," he said. "I appealed to the Commander of the school and he investigated and found the evaluation to not accurately reflect my job performance and it was changed. The senior teaching staff was reamed out by the Commander and I knew my days at the school were numbered. I went to him again and explained the situation and was transferred to New York and assigned to the *USCGC Dallas*.

"The *Dallas* was a very modern ship in every way. She was a 378-foot cutter that had up-to-date mechanical systems. I was on her for two years and learned a great deal. We did a Mediterranean tour, called on France, Spain, England, Nova Scotia, and even did a cross Arctic tour. We did a lot of fishery and drug patrols."

Later, following a two-year stint in Spain, Butch was promoted to Chief (E7) and returned to Yorktown, once again to teach at the machinery tech school. After 3-1/2 years there, he was reassigned to California and the 82-foot patrol boat *Point Bridge*, out of Marina Del Ray. During his two-year tour on the *Point Bridge*, he was commissioned a Chief Warrant Officer. He was sent to New Bedford, Massachusetts, and assigned to the 270-foot *USCGC Campbell*. After three years on the *Campbell*, he was sent to the Mississippi River, where he supervised the operations of seven buoy tenders that worked the river system. He was promoted to the rank of Permanent Warrant Officer Three. His office was in Memphis.

While stationed in Memphis, Butch met his future wife, Cathy. Butch and Cathy, who has two daughters, Loren and Wendi, from a previous marriage, were married in 2002.

After three years in Memphis, Butch retired from active duty in 1996 with twenty years of service. "I would've stayed in the Coast Guard a lot longer, but they retired me for medical reasons," he explained. "I've had a heart problem for a long time. I had my first heart attack at age 28. Since then, there have been additional flare-ups and complications."

Returning home to the Ocean City area, Butch utilized his skills working in the private sector. For five years, he owned his own heating, ventilation, air-conditioning, and refrigeration (HVAC) company named CWO Service. Eventually finding employment with the Worcester County Public Schools, he became a member of their maintenance department. After only one year, he began a teaching assignment at the Worcester Technical High School, near his home.

"In March 2005, a well-liked and effective teacher died while returning home from school," Butch said. "He had been teaching HVAC at the Worcester Technical High School. I was asked, by my supervisor, if I would consider taking over his classes until a replacement was found. I agreed to do this and found the position to be so rewarding that I accepted a permanent full-time position at the school."

While on active duty with the Coast Guard, Butch had earned an Associate of Arts degree from Saint Leo University in Florida. By 2011, he had completed requirements and was awarded a Bachelor's Degree in Career and Technology Education from Wilmington University in nearby Delaware. Currently, he is working toward a Master's Degree from the same institution. At the time this book was being written, he only had five more classes to complete and expected to be awarded this degree in December 2013.

Butch continues to teach HVAC to students at the same school where he graduated in 1975. "Being a teacher has made me a better father, husband, and person," he stated. "The success of my students continues to make me improve my teaching. It has been a very rewarding experience."

Azbell's efforts have not gone unnoticed. In 2008, he was recognized as the National Heating, Ventilation, Air Conditioning, and Refrigeration Teacher of the Year. In 2011, he was named the Worcester Technical High School Teacher of the Year.

During summer vacations, Butch works part-time at a western theme park. "I play a cowboy and rob the train," the affable Azbell laughed. "Sometimes I rob the stagecoach. I've also played an old miner who pans for gold and a drunken judge. From time to time, I also serve as the announcer for the shows."

Butch also has an HVAC business that he does on a part-time basis. He hopes to grow this business after he retires from teaching. He's also a musician, and plays the drums in classic rock, blues, and country bands in the Ocean City area. He also plays drums and sings in his local church, Friendship United Methodist in Berlin, the same church he attended while growing up.

"I feel like my life has gone full-circle," Butch explained. "I've lived in the north and in the south and on both coasts. I've also spent some time in Europe and seen a good portion of the world, but I've always returned home to the Eastern Shore. I guess I have sand between my toes.

"I'm grateful that I moved back here after my years in the Coast Guard. The move was beneficial for my family, especially the girls. Growing up on the Shore has been a lot better for them than growing up in Memphis.

"Through it all, my spirituality has been strong. Divine intervention has guided my life and I am very thankful for it. The two greatest things I've ever done were being a member of the Coast Guard and teaching. I've loved them both. I can't think of a better or more rewarding way to spend a lifetime."

CHAPTER NINE

Hayward Turner

From the time he was toddler, Hayward Turner was involved with seafood. "Several generations of my family owned seafood processing businesses," said Hayward. "I grew up around those plants." The plants were located on the banks of Tarr Creek, just off the Tred Avon River, in the Talbot County town of Bellevue.

Founded by Oswald Tilghman, who named the community in honor of his wife, Patty Belle, Tilghman envisioned the establishment of a resort and spa in Bellevue that would rival Coney Island and Atlantic City. Tilghman's dream never came to fruition, but he is recognized for establishing town boundaries and streets. Some Bellevue citizens dispute the claim that the town was named for Tilghman's wife, however. According to these folks, an early resident of the town, Isabelle Adams, gets credit for being the town's namesake.

"My great-grandfather, William Samuel Turner, was a fascinating man," said Hayward. "In the 1890s, he migrated to Maryland from Kentucky. He was a young man at that point looking for work. In Baltimore, he signed on as a crewmember on a schooner. In a few years, he had gained the skills necessary to qualify as a captain."

The schooner on which Turner crewed made frequent trips to the Eastern Shore. "The schooner hauled freight from Baltimore to the Eastern Shore," Hayward continued. "Bellevue was one of the stops. He delivered freight to the William H. Valliant plant. The schooner also took freight from Bellevue back to Baltimore." Because of his numerous trips to Bellevue, Turner and William H. Valliant became acquainted. Valliant owned a fleet of schooners and offered Turner the position of captain of one of his schooners. Turner accepted and moved into the community.

William H. Valliant owned a great deal of property in the town. He also owned a great deal of property outside the town limits where he raised his own vegetables that he processed in his plant. Bellevue was a company town in those days. Stores, a ship's chandlery, and many houses that were rented to employees were owned by Valliant. The enormous Valliant plant employed the majority of the labor force of the town. By the early 1900s, the plant employed over two hundred crab pickers in the summer and a like number of oyster shuckers during the colder months.

"My grandfather, William A. Turner, had sailed a great deal with his father and had learned the skills necessary to become a captain in his own right," Hayward said. "Like his father, eventually he became a schooner captain and also worked for William H. Valliant. My grandfather was an energetic man who was good-hearted. He would go out of his way to help anyone, he was very generous. He was generally happy and content with his life.

"After World War I, there was a decline in the canning industry. My grandfather decided to go into the seafood-processing business and began shucking oysters in a converted chicken house behind his property. Eventually, he desired to expand his business and build a plant dedicated to processing seafood. He knew that would be difficult since Mr. Valliant owned most of the land in Bellevue. He also needed capital to begin the operation. My father, Samuel E. Turner, had previously worked for the Civilian Conservation Corps and had saved some money. He offered it to his father to be used to purchase land. My grandfather went to Mr. Valliant and offered him the $300 my father had given him. With that, and a promise to pay additional funds in the future, he bought two acres of land on Tarr Creek under the guise of raising chickens to sell eggs. He didn't feel Mr. Valliant would approve of his processing seafood at that location. For a while, my grandfather did raise chickens and sold eggs from the property. At the same time he continued shucking oysters and selling them. My father helped him with the oyster business.

"When World War II broke out, my father was drafted. Following his service during the war he found employment in a shipyard in Pennsylvania. He was a welder at the shipyard. He also went to school and learned drafting, a skill that he would utilize heavily in succeeding years. In 1946, he returned home and entered into a partnership with his father in a seafood processing business named W. A. Turner and Sons. A plant was built on the property that had been purchased from Valliant and the business began operating in 1947."

During the war years, Hayward's mother (Hazel) lived with her parents, Martin and Henrietta Tilghman, on a farm in Deep Neck, near Bellevue. "She had grown-up in an area known as Chapel, not far from Easton," said Hayward. "She and her siblings had to walk several miles each day to get to school. Occasionally, they would take a short-cut across a field. A bull roamed in the field and many days he would chase them and they'd have to run to get by. After graduating from high school, she went to Bowie State College near Baltimore. She was the first person in Bellevue to earn a college degree. She majored in education and taught in Talbot County until her children started coming along. Later, she returned to teaching and worked as a substitute teacher until she was well into her seventies. She passed away in 1993 at the age of eighty-three.

"In 1950, my father and grandfather acquired a skipjack named *Mary F. Crosswell*. She was a large skipjack. She was over seventy-five feet long. They used the boat to dredge for oysters. The oysters they caught were processed at the Turner plant."

Because the Valliant plant employed the majority of the workers in the community, there was a shortage of labor. The resourceful Aubrey Turner traveled to the Somerset County town of Marion Station and recruited workers for his plant. "There were several buildings on the property where the plant was located," said Hayward. "Many of the

Bellevue Seafood, bottom of photo, and
W. A. Turner Seafood, middle of photo.
Courtesy of Hayward Turner.

people that worked there lived in some of those buildings. I don't know if he charged them rent or not. He was a generous man. A great many of the Somerset folks made their permanent home in Bellevue thereafter.

"Fifty to sixty shuckers worked in the plant during oyster season," Hayward continued. "Oyster shuckers could earn about 85 cents for each gallon of oysters they shucked in those days. In the summer, women worked at the plant picking crabs while the men either worked on the water catching crabs or in vegetable processing plants."

In addition to the adult workforce, many neighborhood children also worked in the plant during crabbing season. "Kids cracked claws," said Hayward. "Cracking claws was tedious work and pickers didn't want to be slowed down by having to do that. As a result, many of the women brought along their children to crack claws. The resultant meat would be credited to their parents. I tried cracking claws, but was never very good at it, so I didn't really get into doing it."

Bringing children to crab-processing plants was a common occurrence. The practice took place in just about every crab-processing plant on the Eastern Shore in those days. "Crab pickers earned about 20 cents a pound for the crab meat they picked," said Hayward. "A worker might pick sixty to seventy pounds of crab meat in a day. By 1999, pickers were being paid $1.25 for each pound they picked."

Hayward's dad was responsible for the oyster-shucking operation and his brother, John, was the plant manager and kept the books. W. A. Turner processed crabs in the summer and oysters during the colder months. The business was very successful and remained in operation for many years. By the late 1940s, the Valliant plant had closed.

In the 1950s, Samuel began processing soft-shelled clams in a portion of the W. A. Turner plant. His father and other members of the family did not care to be in the

Bellevue Seafood plant.
Courtesy of Hayward Turner.

clam business. A few years later Samuel split from the W. A. Turner plant. "There were disputes between family members and my father went his separate way," said Hayward. "My grandfather died when I was thirteen, but my uncle and other family members continued to operate the W. A. Turner plant after his death.

"The property on Tarr Creek had been laid out in four parcels and, in 1956, my father built another plant that he named Bellevue Seafood on a neighboring parcel. In addition to oysters, he continued to process soft-shelled clams during the summer at Bellevue Seafood. He was one of the first to get into the clam-processing business in Talbot County. Later, he helped others get into the business. He was very unselfish.

"My father was a consummate business person. He was always trying to improve things in the plant. He was generous and altruistic. He'd go out and buy loads of vegetables and fruit and bring them back to Bellevue and give it away. He did the same in other areas as well. Everybody knew him, he was thought of highly."

Hayward's father built quite a few boats in his backyard that faced the creek. "He was a great builder," said Hayward. "The drafting skills he had learned came in handy as he designed boats and computed their load capacity, waterline location, etc. Eventually, he built about fifteen boats. At over fifty feet, the *Lady Bird* was the largest. Among the other boats he built were *Sarah Regina*, *Davey Crockett*, *Superman*, *William S. Turner*, *William A. Turner* and *Jocko Graves*. They were all utilized in his seafood business.

"*Jocko Graves* had an interesting namesake. I told my father the story of Jocko and he named one of his boats after him. Jocko Graves was the little black boy who was with George Washington as he prepared to cross the Delaware. As the General dismounted his horse, he handed the reins to Jocko. Jocko became somewhat of a celebrity afterwards because of his involvement with the General. All the statues you see today of the young black boy holding the horses reins were supposedly likenesses of Jocko.

"My father ran *William S. Turner*. I crabbed out of a boat named *Muggy*. *Muggy* was built in Oxford, just across the river. Other family members were engaged in running the other boats. In addition to catching oysters and crabs, my father used the *William S. Turner* to catch eels. My brother, Samuel, Jr., worked out of *Jocko Graves* and my other brother, Edzel, worked from the *William A. Turner*. Years later, after the clams died out in the Bay, they took the boats to Crisfield and used them to take out fishing parties during summers. The boats stopped being used by about 2000. By then, they were in poor condition. We burned what remained of the sole-surviving boat just last fall.

"Bellevue Seafood was served primarily by blacks. Many of the watermen who sold their product to the plant were family members. There were six or seven other relatives who owned and operated oystering and clam boats and sold their catch exclusively to Bellevue Seafood.

"I began working there in earnest when I was twelve or thirteen years old. I shucked clams. Quite a few local children worked at the plant as shuckers. Shucking clams was a lot easier than shucking oysters. All that was needed was to cut through the adductor muscle, separate the membrane from the shell, remove the snout, and the clam was ready for processing. Clam shuckers earned sixteen cents a pound in those days." The clams were sold to a plant on Kent Island and they, in turn, would ship them to Massachusetts. Boats were catching between sixty and seventy bushels of clams every day."

Hayward's family lived near the plant. "Our house was right in front of the plant," he laughed. "I used to hang around the plant a lot and catch fish off the wharves. One day I was standing near a set of doors that went into a storage room and a gust of wind blew through and forced the doors open. When the doors opened, they knocked me overboard into the creek. I couldn't swim a stroke. It wasn't a problem, however, because the water was not very deep. I just walked to shore.

"Another time I was in my grandfather's skiff with a group of boys. Grandfather's skiff was very unstable. We were rowing and I fell overboard. I learned really fast how to swim that day because I had to in order to get back to the boat."

Bellevue was a segregated town in those days. About 95% of the townspeople were black; a few whites lived on the fringes of town. "I grew up in a primarily segregated society," Hayward stated. "That was the world I lived in. We lived in our world and the white folks lived in theirs. That's just the way things were in those days. We accepted it as a way of life."

In many ways, segregation negatively affected the Turner family. "My dad couldn't get a loan from a bank," explained Hayward. "Despite the fact that he'd been in business for over twenty years, the bank wouldn't work with him. We couldn't get employment in some institutions just because of the color of our skin.

"In 1972, Hurricane Agnes came through and decimated the clam harvest. My father put in for a government loan to get back on his feet. He had to jump through a lot of hoops while upstarts got loans in no time. There was a definite double-standard. In some cases, those double-standards still exist.

"Bellevue was a swinging town back then. About three hundred people lived in the community. On Friday and Saturday nights Bellevue was a hopping place. My uncle, Nicholas Gardner, owned a store he called Gardner's Hall. On the first floor there was a general store. Upstairs was a large room where meetings, dances, and even movies were shown. Sometimes the upstairs was used as a roller-skating rink. The Mason's later bought the building and used the upstairs for a meeting room. Another building in town housed a beer garden. Bands traveled great distances to play at the establishment, which also hosted floor shows."

There was one church in Bellevue in those days and it served as a focal point for the community. Leaders in the community were also leaders in the church. "St. Luke Methodist Episcopal Church was extremely well attended," said Hayward. "My mother was very active in church activities. She was the long-time secretary for the church. Her mother had been a minister. Her alto voice could be heard on Sundays emanating from the choir loft. Mother was also a wonderful baker and cook. Her Saturday afternoon ritual was baking light bread in the kitchen. She never used a measuring cup during her cooking. If anyone came into our house, she made sure they didn't leave without having a hearty meal. She was a wonderful person.

"Growing up, we were required to go to church services. Every year, during summer vacation, Bible School would be held for two weeks. On the last day, we'd have a party. We also had Easter egg hunts and at Christmas time there'd be a visit from Santa. There would also be a Homecoming once a year. At that time, many people who had moved away would return and attend church. On that day, services would begin at 7 a.m. and continue until 9 that evening. Throughout the day there would be four different services.

"There were lots of community activities that took place in the church. When the elementary school that had formerly been located in Bellevue closed, the church acquired the property and turned it into a hall where dinners were served and many social functions held. In the fall there was a Harvest Home day. Church members brought vegetables and prepared food and people came from all over the county to purchase them. This was a fund-raiser for the church."

Oyster shuckers at Bellevue Seafood.
Courtesy of Hayward Turner.

Hayward attended the Frederick Douglas Elementary School in St. Michaels. During those days, schools were segregated. Blacks attended all-black schools and whites attended all-white schools. For middle and high school, Hayward traveled to Easton and attended R. R. Moton High School, graduating in 1962. Studious, Hayward was a member of the honor society and served as the newspaper editor. He also participated in the Glee Club and band. Hayward was the scorekeeper for the basketball team during his four years of high school.

"My brother, Edzel, is four years older than I and he had been scorekeeper during his years at the school as well," Turner said. "The last day of school was memorable. After school let out for the summer, it seemed like everybody would gather down to the ferry dock (terminus for the Oxford-Bellevue Ferry) and go for a swim. We'd climb up to the top of the pilings and dive off. We'd get on the ferry and ride half-way across the river, then dive off, and swim back to Bellevue. The ferry captain didn't seem to mind our doing this, he was a great guy."

In the late 1950s, Hayward joined the NAACP. "I participated in sit-ins in the '60s," Hayward said. "I attended rallies in Easton at the Asbury Methodist Church. These were supported by the Student Nonviolent Coordinating Committee and the NAACP. They'd divide us up into groups and send us to different establishments. I went up to Easton and, with a group, entered a local restaurant. The owner refused to serve us and called the police. In Maryland, there were trespassing laws on the books in those days and that's how businesses enforced segregation. Police came and took us down to the local jail in Easton and booked us. We went to trial and were found guilty of trespassing, but we never went to jail because our bail was quickly paid and we were freed. Later, the arrest was expunged from our records. My mother was very supportive of the movement. Later on, she even allowed me to use her car to drive to the meetings and activities."

Hayward was very active in the NAACP. Twice, he served as President of the local chapter. "When I was president, we had several meetings with town council members," he explained. "They didn't understand why we weren't willing to wait for things to get better. It seemed like they were only interested in being reelected.

"We also met with the Talbot Board of Education because we thought they were unfairly demoting black school principals following the integration of the school system. A later meeting with the Superintendent of Schools resulted in Martin Luther King Day being declared a holiday for students and school personnel."

Through the years, Hayward has been affiliated with many organizations. Among them are the Talbot Action Group; the Kent, Queen Anne, and Talbot Area Council; the Talbot County Board of Social Services; the Delmarva Advisory Committee; the St. Michaels Elementary-Middle School PTAs; the Bellevue-Royal Oak Community Organization; Talbot County Honor Review Committee; Talbot County Day Care Board; Omega Psi Phi Fraternity; Vietnam Veterans of America; and Veterans of Foreign Wars and Nomads of Annapolis. Hayward was also a member of the Talbot County Charter Committee, serving as its co-chairman. He made an unsuccessful bid for county commissioner in 1972.

"I never thought I'd see the day when a black person would be elected President of the United States," he said. "Many thought he was going to do miracles, I never did. He's only one man and he has to work with a hostile Congress that puts up many blockades. The whole system is controlled by lobbyists."

Graduating from college in 1966 (Morgan State College in Baltimore) with a degree in science education, Hayward entered the Army and was commissioned a second lieutenant. "I never did teach," he said. "Instead, I was sent to Germany and later Vietnam."

Hayward was a chemical officer in Vietnam. "I commanded a chemical detachment," he explained. "One of our missions was to go out on sniffer patrols. Sniffer patrols involved flying in a helicopter about fifty to sixty feet above the jungle. We had a machine on board that sampled the air. The machine could detect the presence of ammonia or smoke. When the needle went off, we knew there were people in that spot. We'd report 'hot spot,' 'hot spot' over the radio and another helicopter flying above us would note the position. Later, an air strike might follow.

"We handled Agent Orange, a substance used to defoliate the jungle. We didn't know how dangerous the stuff was. Sometimes the drums it was stored in would leak and we'd get it on our hands and clothing. We also constructed and installed perimeter defense systems made from napalm and high explosives. In the event that the enemy attacked, the defense system would be ignited."

Hayward served in Vietnam for a one-year tour. In September 1969, following his time there, he was discharged with the rank of Captain. For his dedicated service, Hayward received the National Defense Medal, Vietnam Campaign Medal, Army Air Medal with Oak Leaf Cluster, Army Commendation Medal, Vietnam Service Medal, and the Bronze Star.

"I had a rough time adjusting to civilian life at first," he said. "If a low-flying jet flew over, I'd hit the ground for cover. The sound it made reminded me of a rocket. If I heard loud noises, I would jump. It took me a while to return to normal."

In 1969, Hayward returned home and began working at Bellevue Seafood as the Plant Manager. "I oversaw the daily operations of the plant," he said. "Shucking, packing, shipping were all part of my responsibility. My father dealt with bringing the product into the plant. My oldest brother, Edzel, kept the books. My youngest brother, Samuel, Jr., caught the product and also helped out around the plant. (My sister Regina never worked in the plant. She is a college professor in Indiana.) We had four trucks and we shipped oysters all over the shore and to Virginia. We shipped out about 250 gallons of oysters each day. When we were processing crabs, we shipped hundreds of bushels daily. We shipped our clams to Massachusetts. In about 1990 or '92, we got out of processing clams and, from then on, processed only crabs and oysters."

Bellevue Seafood ceased operating in 1999. After thirty years, the closing of the plant ended Haywood's affiliation. The dwindling supply of oysters and clams was a major influence in the decision to close. The shortage of labor was also a factor and it was increasingly difficult to compete with the larger processors in the marketplace. Shortly after closing the plant, Hayward's father died. He was eighty-nine when he died in 2001.

Following the closing of Bellevue Seafood, Hayward found employment near Chestertown, in the Kent County town of the same name. Chestertown Foods deboned and diced chicken and processed chicken fat and chicken stock. They sold their product to a variety of companies, but primarily to Campbell's soups. Hayward was the second shift supervisor. He worked there until 2008. He had reached retirement age and his health was also a factor.

In the late 1990s, Hayward developed congestive heart failure. "I firmly believe it was related to my exposure to Agent Orange when I was in the Army," he said. "It takes up to thirty years for Agent Orange to affect some people after exposure. It affects people in different ways. Some get cancer; others get heart disease or diabetes. There are thirteen diseases linked to Agent Orange exposure. I didn't file a claim with the Veteran's Administration until 2005. They turned me down initially and refused to help me. They said my condition was not the type that was brought on by exposure to Agent Orange. I'm in the process of appealing that decision presently."

PERISHABLE
KEEP REFRIGERATED

BELLEVUE SEAFOOD CO.
BELLEVUE BOX 58
ROYAL OAK, MD. 21662
MD 262 SP

FRESH OYSTERS SHUCKED DAILY WITH THE GREATEST
CARE GIVEN TO CLEANLINESS AND SANITATION.

SEE LID FOR SIZE DESIGNATION

FRESH
OY

Container in which Bellevue oysters were shipped.

Married since 1977, Hayward has a daughter, Kamesha Lanee, who is 31. "She lives in Denton and is a Physician's Assistant," he said with pride. "My wife, Yolanda, works in Salisbury for the Employment Security division of the Department of Labor and Licensing."

Hayward is concerned about the health of the Chesapeake Bay. "The Chesapeake Bay is in terrible shape," he said. "It's a far cry from the Bay I remember when I was growing up. There was so much eel grass in Tarr Creek in those days that there was only a twenty-foot opening that would allow boats to get through. Eel grass was so abundant that we could catch soft crabs all around the shoreline. Now the eel grass is all gone. There aren't any more oysters either. Over at the lighthouse the water was so clear that you could see thirty-five feet below the surface. No longer can you do that.

"The Chesapeake Bay is so far beneath what it once was that it will take a Herculean effort to clean it up. It's not just a Maryland-Virginia problem. The watershed reaches all the way up into New York. What folks do up there has an effect on the Bay. I'm skeptical if it'll ever be any better."

The building that once housed Bellevue Seafood was purchased and converted into a large waterfront residence. Only the jagged fragments of a foundation and pilings remain from the W. A. Turner plant.

"I've lived an eventful life," said Hayward. "I wouldn't change anything; I'm satisfied with my life. My greatest source of satisfaction is thinking back on my relationship with the shuckers and pickers with whom I associated. They were sincere, hardworking people who would do anything for you. Seldom did they complain; they were willing workers who came to work with smiles on their faces and joy in their hearts. They were very appreciative of any kindnesses shown them. Those were good days."

CHAPTER TEN

Lloyd L. Simpkins

On an unseasonably warm June afternoon, Lloyd L. Simpkins sat in a gazebo next to his Somerset County home not far from the banks of the Wicomico River. A corncob pipe was seldom withdrawn from his lips and an ample supply of his favorite tobacco was within easy reach. As he spoke, his remarks were frequently punctuated by the direction of his pipe. The circular gazebo was filled with the conveniences he most desired; a cooler was well-stocked and a television set was located in such a position that enabled easy viewing of his favorite baseball teams, the Saint Louis Cardinals and the Baltimore Orioles. Nearby were the trailboards (intricately carved boards attached to either side of the bow of a boat that display the name of the vessel) from his beloved skipjack, *Good Intent*. A ceiling fan whirled above his head, cooling the gazebo and keeping the infamous Somerset mosquitoes at bay. He spoke in an authoritative, no-nonsense manner, a result of the many years he served in the political arena and on the judicial bench.

Simpkins has resided in this area for the entirety of his ninety-two years. "My family has lived here since the 1770s," he said. "We were dirt poor when I was growing up. A family couldn't get much poorer than we were, but everybody was poor back then; it was during the Depression. If your dad was fortunate enough to have a job, he was lucky if he made ten cents an hour.

"I had seven brothers and sisters and, of those, six lived to adulthood. All of us that survived have met with some success. I had one brother who was probably the most able one of the bunch. He had more on the ball than any of the rest of us. Unfortunately, he was an alcoholic and that took its toll. You could take a bottle of liquor and lead him all the way to Cape Charles if you wanted to."

Simpkins' father, a waterman, owned a bugeye named *Joseph Faulkner*. "The *Faulkner* was seventy or seventy-five feet long and she was built in the Cambridge/Oxford area by a man named Joseph Faulkner who named the boat for himself," said Lloyd. "My father hauled freight all over the Bay in the boat when he wasn't in her dredging for oysters

Lloyd Simpkins relaxing in his gazebo. Note the trailboards and name board from his skipjack.

during winters. In warmer weather, he hauled hay, tomatoes — anything that didn't require cold storage. I used to go with him on short trips. I guess that's where I got my love for sailing."

Eventually, the elder Simpkins established the Simpkins Packing Company, an oyster-processing operation. "He was involved with the Simpkins Packing Company for many years," Lloyd said. "Dad ran the oyster house until 1946. When the school bus brought me home, I'd go in the house, change my clothes, and go down to the oyster house. I'd clean up the area where the oyster shuckers had worked that day. I did this during my high school years."

The oyster house was located near Simpkins' current home. He and his bother purchased the 150-acre parcel in the late 1940s. Through the years, it has become a family compound of sorts. Some of his nephews, as well as his daughter, reside on the property.

"My dad gave me a nickname when I was two years old," he said. "He called me 'Hot Dog.' I have no idea why he called me that, don't have a clue. Everybody I know calls me by my nickname. Very few refer to me by my real name. Dad also gave me my name, Lloyd Lewis. He said I was named for a man who owed him lots of money and he never wanted to forget him.

"My dad lived to be 89. He was blind by then and during his last days we had to put him in a nursing home in Salisbury. The day we took him to the home to be admitted was Election Day. When he got to his room, he discovered that he had a roommate. It turned out that his roommate was a political enemy from Pocomoke. There were two factions in the Democratic Party in those days. Dad belonged to one faction and his roommate the other. They couldn't get along with each other at all, never could. The two of them got into a fist-fight and dad had to be moved to another room. He died the very next day.

"My mother was a very bright woman. She was the best read woman I've ever been around. She taught school part-time until the kids started coming along. She really was the central force that held our family together. She and my dad were married for sixty years or more."

Born in 1920, a half-mile from his present home, Simpkins attended school in the Somerset County hamlet of Mount Vernon through grade six. "I was a terrible student," he said. "I had dyslexia when I was a young kid and had trouble reading. I flunked the first grade and had to repeat it. Eventually, though, I outgrew my dyslexia." Even though he had dyslexia, Lloyd enjoyed school and the learning process. "I knew early on that I wanted to go to college," he continued. "I always just assumed that I would eventually attend college."

For the upper grades, Hot Dog attended schools in Princess Anne, ultimately graduating from the high school there. "I spent an extra year in high school," he stated. "That's because I was working part-time in a service station in Princess Anne. I earned ten cents an hour on that job."

Following high school, Simpkins matriculated at the University of Maryland, College Park. Athletic and sports-minded, he played on the University baseball team. "I made the team, but I seldom played because I couldn't hit," Lloyd said. "There were two guys on the team, though, that were good enough to eventually play professional ball — Charlie Keller and Pershing Mondorff."

Keller was signed by the New York Yankees in 1937. In a 1939 World Series game, he hit five home runs. An outfielder, Keller would also play for Detroit. His playing days lasted until 1952. He died in 1990 at age seventy-three. Pershing Mondorff was a four-sport star at the University of Maryland. In addition to baseball, he also played basketball, football, and soccer. Mondorff played Triple A baseball with the Montreal Royals of the International League. Both Mondorff and Keller are members of the University of Maryland's Athletic Hall of Fame.

During Lloyd's days as a student at Maryland, the President of the University was Dr. Harry C. (Curly) Byrd, a Somerset County native (Crisfield) who had worked himself up through the ranks to become the leader of one of the largest university systems in the world. He was president of the University from 1936 until 1954. "Byrd was with the University for a very long time," said Simpkins. "I'd go to his office before classes started for the semester and sign a note in order to pay my tuition and fees. There were hundreds of boys doing that, not just me. When I was a student, tuition was $110 a year. I worked in the dining hall to pay my room and board. Meals cost 35 cents in those days."

During his own student days at the University, Byrd was quite an athlete. As the quarterback on the football team, he was one of the first players in the east to perfect the forward pass. He also played baseball and ran track. Following graduation, he was hired as the football coach. The stadium where the University football team now plays is named in his honor. He was also a pitcher in the minor leagues. In 1982, Byrd was inducted into the University of Maryland Athletic Hall of Fame. The colorful Byrd was a cousin of former Governor, J. Millard Tawes, another Crisfield native. Following his service at the University, Byrd was appointed Commissioner of Tidewater Fisheries, forerunner to the Department of Natural Resources. He later made an unsuccessful bid for governor.

During Hot Dog's third year of college, Japan attacked Pearl Harbor and World War II resulted. "Japan bombed Pearl Harbor on December 7, 1941…I joined the Navy the very next day," said Simpkins. "I felt it was my duty to go to war…it was the right thing to do."

Lloyd was in the Navy for five years. He enlisted as a seaman. "I was a tail gunner on a dive bomber in the South Pacific," he said. "We flew off the carrier *Enterprise* and also from Henderson Field on Guadalcanal. I also flew from Ford Island on Hawaii. I was sent there not long after the attack on Pearl Harbor. If you could go there and see all that desolation without shedding a tear, there was something wrong with you. That was a heartbreaking scene. I eventually attended flight school and became a pilot and an officer. I served in the South Pacific from 1942 through 1945. When I left the Navy, I was an ensign."

Following his naval career, Judge Simpkins continued to fly airplanes. "I continued flying small planes after the war," he said. "I'd go to Salisbury and rent a plane from 'Sunshine' Rayne for $8 an hour. I enjoyed flying over the Bay and looking down on it. Flying and sailing were two of my favorite activities. They were both a lot of fun.

"By the time I left the Navy, I had paid off my prior debt to Dr. Byrd at the University of Maryland. I was discharged from the Navy in February of 1946 and the very next day resumed my studies at College Park. I graduated from the University of Maryland with a Bachelor of Science degree later that same year.

"With benefits from the G. I. Bill, I bought the oyster house back home. My dad was tired of running the place so I bought it. I ran it for two years after I graduated from College Park and then brought in Hopkins Fisher as a partner. After Hop joined the business, I went to law school, something I had always wanted to do.

"I was fascinated by the law and by government. I loved all levels of government — local, state, and federal. Liked them all, always have and always will. That was in 1949. Eventually, I sold out my part of the business to my partner and he ran the place for the next fifty years. I graduated from the University of Maryland School of Law in 1952."

Following law school, Lloyd and his younger brother, Tom, established a law practice in Princess Anne. "Tom was a good man," said Hot Dog. "He was two years behind me in law school. After he graduated, he practiced in Salisbury for a couple of years before coming to Princess Anne and joining me in a law practice. Our firm was called Simpkins and Simpkins and we concentrated on the general practice of law. When Tom was sixty years old, he developed a brain tumor and died. His son, Kirk, is now involved with the practice." During those years, Lloyd served as the attorney for the town of Princess Anne. He was also the attorney for the Somerset County Liquor Board.

In 1951, while still in law school, Simpkins was elected to the Maryland House of Delegates, representing Somerset County. He ultimately served for eight years in the House. "The Eastern Shore was politically very powerful in those days," he explained. "Those were the days before redistricting occurred. Every county in the state was represented in the Senate and the House. Somerset had three members in the House. Along with southern Maryland, the Eastern Shore delegation could control the state politically because we had the majority of representatives.

"During the legislative session, a bunch of us lived in a rooming house in Annapolis. One of the fellows would wake us up each morning by banging a garbage can on the floor. One day I caught him in the bathroom sitting on the john and loaded a garbage can full of cherry bombs (a type of fire cracker). I lit them and pushed them inside the bathroom. He was more careful with the way he woke us after that."

In the House of Delegates, Simpkins was named chairman of the Agricultural Committee. He served in this capacity from 1951 until 1955. In 1955, he was appointed Chairman of the Judiciary Committee, a position he held until 1959.

"I consider my time as Chair of the Judiciary Committee my greatest accomplishment in Annapolis," Simpkins said. "Every bill that went through the legislature went through the Judiciary Committee. No less than six members of that committee would go on to high office. Future United States Senators Brewster, Tydings, and Beal served on the committee. Blair Lee, Marvin Mandel, and Harry Hughes also served on the committee and would go on to become Governors of the state of Maryland. We did a good job. Former Governor Harry Hughes remains one of my closest friends to this day. He is very bright, a decent man — a good man."

Hughes, from the Eastern Shore county of Caroline, served in the House of Delegates with Simpkins from 1955 through 1959. He was elected to the Maryland Senate in 1959 and remained until 1971, when he was appointed Secretary of Transportation. In 1979, he was elected Governor and served until 1987. Hughes was a strong advocate for the preservation of the Chesapeake Bay and signed the first Chesapeake Bay Agreement, an early initiative to restore the Bay.

From 1955 until 1959, Simpkins served on the Legislative Council. In 1959, he resigned from the House to become the Executive Assistant to then-Governor J. Millard Tawes. "There was no such position as Lieutenant Governor in those days, but my job was very similar to that position," he said. In 1961, the Governor appointed him to the position of Secretary of State. He served in that role until the end of Tawes' term in 1967.

"Governor Tawes and I were very close friends," Lloyd stated. "He was a good man, but he was tighter than hell. One year he invited me over to the Governor's Mansion to watch the All-Star (baseball) Game. He was quite a baseball fan. He didn't have a TV so he made inquiries about renting one to watch the game. He was told that it would cost $8 an hour. He pitched a fit and refused to rent a set. He said that we could get into the ballpark to watch the game cheaper than it would cost to rent a TV. 'I know we can Governor,' I told him, 'but the ball park is in Pittsburgh.' It ended up that Tawes and I were the only two that didn't see the game that year."

Hot Dog explained that Tawes had no legislative experience when he became Governor. Tawes was elected Clerk of Court in Somerset County in 1938. A few years later he became the Comptroller of the Treasury for the state and then Governor. Following his service in the Governor's office, he became Secretary of Natural Resources. He was also Secretary of the Treasury at one time. "He held every high office he could under the Maryland Constitution except Attorney General," said Hot Dog. "He couldn't hold that office because he wasn't a lawyer; he had a business degree."

Simpkins went on to explain that Tawes was a fiscal conservative. "Finance was his area of expertise," he continued. "One year he gave back $150,000 or $200,000 from the Governor's office that he hadn't spent — that was unheard of at the time. If four or five of us in the office had to work late, we'd often go out to dinner together. After we'd eaten, the Governor would inquire about how much each person's dinner cost and then, when the check came, he'd collect that amount from each person present. He didn't believe in wasting money."

During his long political career, the Judge rubbed elbows with lots of famous politicians. "I had dinner with John F. Kennedy once," he stated. "He was in Annapolis a lot. We went to his house for dinner. I liked him, he was a good man. I also knew his brother, Bobby. He was a bit arrogant, I thought. His other brother, Ted, seemed to me to be the most capable of the lot. He was a good man. I also knew Lyndon Johnson. He was a first-rate horse's ass. He looked out for only one person — himself.

"At the state level, I knew several former Governors. In addition to Tawes, Hughes, Mandell, and Lee, I also knew McKeldon. He was a phony, but I liked him. Lane was a good man. I also knew Agnew, Glendenning, and William Donald Schaefer."

The Judge is skeptical of the way things are going in Washington, D.C. "We've got some real problems at the federal level," he said. "I'm not impressed with our President. I was an old Roosevelt man. I liked FDR and his politics. When Harry Truman came into office, I didn't think he was worth a damn. Now, though, I think he was one of the best Presidents we've ever had."

As far as the state is concerned, Simpkins has positive feelings. "Maryland is in good shape," he continued. "We live in one of the wealthiest states in the Union as far as per capita wealth is concerned. The Maryland Constitution says that we've got to have a balanced budget every year. Maryland is the only state in the Union that has this requirement. I think that is a great thing to have. We'd be in a lot less trouble if other states and the federal government had similar requirements."

Lloyd was married in 1957 to a local girl, the former Betty Wilson. The couple has a daughter who has been a Judge of the Probate Court in Somerset County for twenty-five years. In 1971, Simpkins was appointed by Governor Mandel to the bench. At first, he served as a judge in the District Court and later the Circuit Court, where he served until his retirement in 1990.

"My service in the District Court was pretty much limited to Somerset County, but Circuit Court covered Dorchester, Wicomico, Worcester, and Somerset Counties," Judge Simpkins said. "I sat through some memorable cases. My most memorable case involved a little ten-year-old girl. The case had been transferred down here from Baltimore. The girl's parents had kept her locked in a closet since she was eight years old. There was very little light in the closet and she was given just enough food to survive. It was a terrible situation. I sentenced her father to forty-seven years and her mother to thirty-six years. I also gave the death penalty to thirteen people. One man killed six people and another murdered four. The man who killed six was twenty-one years old and a college student at the time. He had been in jail off and on since he was nine years old. He said that he killed the first of the six men because he liked them. His parents were very honorable people. A shame, really."

In 1949, Hot Dog had a 38-foot skipjack built. "If you counted the thirteen-foot bowsprit, the boat was fifty-one feet long," Lloyd explained. "I named the boat *Good Intent*. I ran across those words somewhere in my reading and thought they would make an appropriate name for a boat. She was built by a man named Shores over in Oriole. I covered quite a bit of the Bay in that boat."

In 1969, the Judge sold the *Good Intent* and had a two-masted skipjack built for his use. "She was sixty-seven feet overall, forty-five feet on deck, and she had a draft of seven feet with the centerboard down and three feet when it was up," Simpkins continued. "She was built just outside of Cambridge by Jim Richardson. Richardson was a master builder who had a terrific reputation for building boats; he was a crackerjack, one of the best in the country. He did a lot of work for the Smithsonian. The next boat he built after mine was the *Dove*, a replica of the historic ship that first brought settlers to the state of Maryland. Ever since she was built, the *Dove* has been on display over in St. Mary's City. I named my second boat *Good Intent* also. The second *Good Intent* was fully equipped; she had a diesel engine, electric heat, air-conditioning, hot and cold running water, a generator, TV, and all the conveniences of home. She even had a shower. She could sleep six. Once, Betty and I spent every weekend on the boat for an entire year. We even spent Christmas on the boat."

Lloyd Simpkins at helm of *Good Intent*.
Courtesy of Lloyd L. Simpkins.

Simpkins had a slip (berth) at the Kent Island Yacht Club. From there, it was a short hop to the Bay. "I sailed the latter *Good Intent* all over the Chesapeake Bay," he said. "I even ventured up the Delaware River to Philadelphia. I also went up the Hudson as far as Lake Geneva. I never sailed further south than the Chesapeake Bay Bridge Tunnel, though, and didn't go out into the ocean."

Simpkins' wife, Betty, explained that when he was a judge, Hot Dog was often called upon to go to other counties to try cases. She would accompany him when he

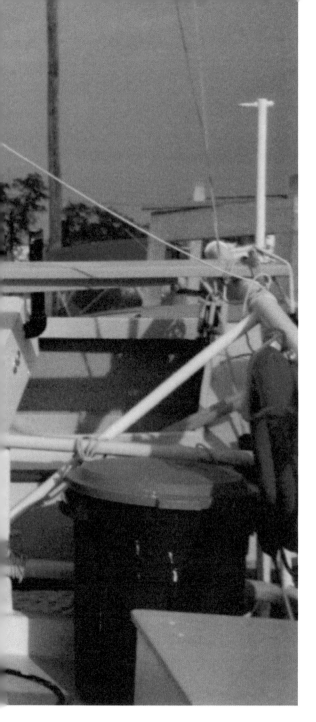

traveled by boat. "I remember staying at the Solomons Yacht Club for a month while he covered Circuit Court over in Calvert County," she said. "A friend loaned him a car so he could get back and forth from the courthouse to the boat. While we were there, Jimmy Dean (a country singer turned sausage baron) came in and tied up not far from our boat. Walter Cronkite was an honorary member of the club also. He had been there in his boat shortly before we got there. That was shortly before Hot Dog retired."

Betty recounted one particular harrowing trip from Kent Island to Mount Vernon. "We set out for home from Kent Island one day," she said. "The weather didn't look good when we left, but we were anxious to get home. We didn't have the radio on and missed warnings that tornados were forecast for the Bay. As we sailed down the Bay, the boat was heeled over so much from the force of the wind that our ankles were wet as water came over the side of the boat while we stood on deck. We were the only boat out on the Bay. Our daughter, who was with us, was only nine years old at the time and she thought the trip was a lot of fun."

Simpkins kept the boat until about seven years ago. "I couldn't find anybody to work on the boat and she needed lots of work," he said. "It seemed like everything had gone to fiberglass by then and few people worked on wooden boats. For a while I tried to sell her, but when that was not successful I gave her to the owner of the local marina. He stripped her of everything that was useful and then burned her up."

The Chesapeake is not the pristine Bay he remembers during his childhood. "The Chesapeake Bay has been going to hell since I was old enough to read," he said. "It seems like it never improves. You've got to have oysters — oysters filter the water. One oyster will filter eighty gallons of water a day. At one time there were fifteen million bushels of oysters a year caught in the Bay — that's a lot of oysters — and the Bay was much cleaner than it is today. Today, oysters only live about three years, then disease hits them and they die. It wasn't that way years ago; they lived a whole lot longer.

"One thing the Tawes Administration did was to plant seed (young) oysters each year in order to propagate the oyster population. Under Tawes and Dr. Byrd, when

Skipjack *Good Intent. Courtesy of Lloyd L. Simpkins.*

he was the head of the Tidewater Fisheries, about six million bushels were planted each year. They do very little of that anymore. You've got to have oysters if you want a clean Bay."

In addition to spending lots of time in his gazebo, Judge Simpkins travels to Princess Anne nearly every morning to meet with a group of cronies. "I meet with a bunch of old farts and we sit around and talk," he smiled as he relit his pipe. "I usually go up there, get an argument started, and then I get up and go home.

"Corncob pipes are all I've smoked for the last fifty years or so. Corncobs don't require a great deal of time to break in. Most pipes have to be smoked for some time before they are broken in. Not so with corncobs. You can't get a decent corncob pipe anymore. The corn growers continue to develop cobs with increasing numbers of kernels. Those extra kernels ruined the corncob pipe. You can't get a good one anymore."

Hot Dog is well practiced in the art of telling tall tales. When speaking about the Somerset County weather, he has been heard to say, "A nor'easter went through here the other day and it was so strong that it blew a sitting hen into a two gallon bottle." He also recounted that winds blew so hard one week that Wednesday didn't arrive until Friday.

Judge Lloyd "Hot Dog" Simpkins has no regrets about his life. "I've loved the law, all levels of government, and all branches of government," he said. "I've never had a job in my life that I didn't enjoy. I also can't think of anybody I've met that I disliked. That's very fortunate, I think. It's been a good life and I have no regrets."

Epilogue: Sadly, since the compilation of this book, Betty Simpkins has passed away. Her wit, wisdom, and remembrances live on.

CHAPTER ELEVEN

Eddie E. Somers, Jr.

Eddie E. Somers, Jr. at the helm of *J. Millard Tawes*.

The big diesels in the one-hundred-foot buoy tender, *J. Millard Tawes*, revved in response to Capt. Eddie Somers' commands. The *Tawes* slowly moved into the position that Somers demanded and he gave the order to lower the spuds. Down on the deck, a crewmember pressed a button and the 26-foot-tall spuds were hydraulically lowered into the muddy bottom of Tangier Sound, temporarily making the *Tawes* immobile.

The arm of a five-ton crane was maneuvered over the targeted buoy as it floated alongside the starboard bow of the *Tawes*. A crewmember looped a length of chain around the buoy, attached it to the crane, and the barnacle-encrusted buoy was effortlessly lifted aboard. The anchor chain, attached to the buoy noisily, announced its arrival on the steel deck with a rhythmic staccato. "See that weight attached to the chain on the underside of the buoy?" the soft-spoken Somers pointed. "That chunk of concrete weighs between eight hundred and nine hundred pounds. You can see by the markings just how far into the muddy bottom the weight was submerged."

Once aboard, the buoys were stored and fresh anchor chains were attached to newly-refurbished buoys. The new buoys were lifted from the deck and entered Tangier Sound in the exact location where the originals had been. Buoys that were lifted from the bottom would later be taken to Crisfield to be refurbished by the *Tawes*' crew in an extensive shop on the grounds of the Somers Cove Marina. Thereafter, they are stored until once again needed as replacement buoys.

The state buoy tender, *J. Millard Tawes*, was on a routine mission in Holland Straits, an area in Tangier Sound. Its task, on that chilly March day, was to remove and replace the buoys that mark the boundary between the counties of Somerset and Dorchester. "Crabbers will soon be needing these markers in order to know exactly where to place

Buoy tender *J. Millard Tawes.*
Courtesy of Eddie E. Somers, Jr.

their crab pots," Capt. Somers said. "This section of Dorchester County doesn't allow crabpots. These buoys show crabbers where that boundary is located."

Capt. Somers and his crew are responsible for the maintenance of approximately three hundred buoys from the Honga River southward to the Virginia state line on the Eastern Shore, as well as state-controlled buoys in the Patuxent and Potomac Rivers. They also maintain buoys in Assawoman Bay, near Ocean City.

"We aren't responsible for federal navigational buoys," Somers stated. "They are maintained by the United States Coast Guard. We're responsible only for state navigational buoys and those that mark boundaries. We also take care of buoys that mark clamming and restricted areas. About 150 day beacons are our responsibility as well. We change the boards and refurbish them as needed."

Capt. Somers explained that the *Tawes* averages replacing about fifteen buoys per day depending on travel time and location of the buoys. "Sometimes we have to spend the night," he said. "Particularly when we work the upper reaches of the Potomac. We're a long way from home when we work there." Eddie said that the crew anchors the boat for the night when such trips are necessary. "We just put down the spuds and the boat will usually stay put for the night."

In addition to tending Chesapeake buoys, the *Tawes* and her counterparts in the upper Bay break ice when required. "The bottom of the *Tawes* is 3/8-inch steel and the hull sides are 1/4-inch steel," said Eddie. "Breaking ice is a really good service we provide. The people on Smith Island, for example, depend on us to keep the channel

Buoy being lifted aboard the *J. Millard Tawes*;
note the spud in the lowered position.

clear. The *Tawes* is rated as being able to break ice as thick as seventeen inches. We've actually broken ice that is thicker than that."

The *Tawes* was built in Debuque, Iowa, in 1942 for the United States Coast Guard. Originally named *Barberry*, she was used as a buoy tender. Weighing in at 178 tons, with a beam in excess of twenty-four feet and nearly a six-foot draft, she was

launched in November of 1942. Powered by twin six-cylinder diesels, the *Barberry* cruised in the eight- to ten-knot range. More recently, a pair of 500-horsepower diesels was installed.

When the *Tawes* was the property of the Coast Guard, she carried a crew of seventeen. The entire crew lived aboard the vessel. Today, the boat carries a crew of four, including Capt. Somers. Lee Daniels, grandson of legendary skipjack captain Art Daniels, serves as mate; Wardell Fennell, a retired U. S. Navy boatswains mate, is classified as a sailor; and Ozzie Wilkinson is the engineer. "The *Tawes* can hold 2,500 gallons of fresh water and 3,800 gallons of diesel fuel," Capt. Eddie explained.

In the early 1970s, when the *Barberry* was declared surplus by the Coast Guard, the state of Maryland purchased the boat for the tidy sum of $100. In addition to the Crisfield-based *Tawes*, two other buoy tenders were built for the Maryland fleet: the *Widener* is based in Cambridge and serves Maryland's middle portion of the Bay and the *Sandusky*, based in Matapeake, takes care of buoys in the upper Chesapeake. The boats are all of similar design and built to state standards.

Each of the stations is also assigned an outboard-powered vessel that is equipped with a 250-pound capacity, electrically-powered crane in order to work the shallows when access is prohibited by the larger vessel's draft. The 23-foot boat assigned to the Crisfield station regularly works the waters near Ocean City.

Never far from the Chesapeake, Eddie Somers grew up on Smith Island. "My great-great-grandfather, James Somers, was the assistant lighthouse keeper on the Kedges Straits Lighthouse in the 1870s," said Eddie with his characteristic Smith Island accent. "Eventually, he was promoted to chief keeper."

James had a son, Daniel, who married a girl from Smith Island and settled there. "His son, Daniel, Jr., was my grandfather," Eddie said. "My dad, Edward, Sr., lived on the island and, like his grandfather and father before him, worked on the water." Eddie, Sr. was a crab scraper during the crabbing season. "My dad worked with his

Breaking ice aboard the *J. Millard Tawes*. Courtesy of Eddie E. Somers, Jr.

father on a skipjack during oyster season. When he was a kid, he worked on the skipjack *Eldora*. His father gave him a 1/2-share at the end of the season. The other crewmembers tried to get my grandfather to give him a full share like the rest of the crew received, but grandfather refused to do that." Shares aboard skipjacks were calculated in thirds. After the food bill was paid, the remaining money earned during dredging season was split by giving the captain a third, the boat a third (for upkeep), and the crew the remaining third.

"Dad worked on a couple of other skipjacks later on," Eddie continued. "He sailed on the *Somerset* with Capt. Elmer Evans and also the *Lorraine Rose* with Capt. Clyde Evans. Life aboard skipjacks was not easy in those days. After the fleet went out at the start of the oyster season in the fall, they didn't return home until Christmas. Thanksgiving was never a big holiday on the island like it was on the mainland. That's because the men weren't around to help celebrate. After Christmas, the skipjacks went out again and we wouldn't see them until spring. They'd anchor out at night and sell their catch to buyboats."

Eddie, Jr. was born in 1956 and grew up on Smith Island. His parents, Eugene Edward and Lorraine Somers, along with Eddie's two older sisters, Beverly and Debbie, resided in the town of Ewell. Eddie remained on the island until he married at age twenty-five. "Growing up on Smith Island was like living a Huckleberry Finn existence," said Eddie with a twinkle in his eye. "I really enjoyed living there. We were free to roam about the island; swimming in the creeks, netting for crabs, fishing, hunting, and searching for arrowheads…It was a wonderful childhood. Smith Island was a close-knit community, everybody knew everybody — we couldn't get away with anything."

Eddie described a community where doors were seldom locked and citizens felt safe and secure. "Our homes were not air-conditioned when I was growing up," he said. "We'd sleep with the windows open in the summer. I remember lying in bed and listening to the wind blowing through the trees. We had a silver dollar poplar tree near the windows and the leaves would rattle when the wind blew through them. I really miss hearing those sounds and I miss those days. Being on the island was contentment. It was a good life."

When he was ten or twelve years old, Eddie became the proud owner of a sixteen-foot skiff that was powered by a six-horsepower outboard motor. "I used it to progue (explore) around in the marshes and netting crabs in the summer," he laughed. "I made my very first dollar in that skiff. I caught about a dozen hard crabs that day and was paid a dollar for them. When I got home, my dad took the dollar I had earned, reached into his wallet, and gave me a dollar in its place. Later, he gave me the original dollar plus the sales ticket. I still have that dollar at home."

In the winter, he used the skiff to hunt geese and ducks. "I hunted a lot when I lived on the island," Eddie said. "One day my friends, John Tyler and Larry Marsh, and I took Johnny's skiff and poled up a marsh gut to the hunting grounds. We snubbed the bow of the skiff up on a mud bank and went hunting. When we returned, the tide had fallen and we had to cross a wide, muddy gut to get to the boat. Tyler lost one of his boots, and one of the boys lost their gun. I stepped out of my boots. It was a mess."

Eddie attended elementary and middle school on Smith Island. "The school in Ewell had four rooms," he said. "Kindergartners had their own room and grades 1 through 3 were in another. Grades four, five, and six were in a room and the seventh and eighth grades were together in another room. There were about one hundred kids in the school back then. Now there are probably less than a dozen."

For high school, Eddie traveled to Crisfield and attended Crisfield High School. "I wasn't much of a student," he continued. "I really didn't want to go to high school, but my parents made me go. High school students traveled to Crisfield on the mail boat, *Island Star*, early Monday morning. It took an hour and twenty minutes to reach Crisfield. In Crisfield, we had to stay with a family during the week. The county paid for our room and board. On Friday, we were taken back to Smith Island. During our trips on the *Island Star*, the boys would play poker in the forepeak. I graduated from high school in 1974." Today, high school students travel to Crisfield daily on a high-speed catamaran. The boat is the only school boat in Maryland and, undoubtedly, one of the few in the country.

During the summer, while still in high school, Eddie crabbed with a Smith Island waterman named Edward Jones. He worked with him for two years, crab potting and scraping.

Following graduation, Somers worked as a mate on a buyboat named *Juanita* for a year. The *Juanita*, about fifty feet in length, regularly traveled to the Patuxent and Potomac Rivers to buy oysters. "We ran our oysters to a buyer located on the Coan River, up in the Patuxent," Eddie said. "One night we were coming around Point Lookout and the wind was blowing a gale from the northwest. I was asleep in my bunk and the Captain woke me up. I asked, 'What's the matter?' He said that nothing was wrong; he just woke me in case something was to happen. I was young then and didn't take the situation seriously and went back to bed. If that happened to me today, I'd be scared to death."

Shortly after his buyboat experience, Eddie signed on as a crewmember aboard the skipjack *Martha Lewis*, which was owned at the time by Gene Tyler. "We were home every weekend in those days," Eddie said. "It was cold on the boats and the conditions were rather primitive. It wasn't an easy life out there." Still sailing today, the *Martha Lewis* is forty-six feet in length with a beam of seventeen feet. She carried a crew of five inclusive of the Captain.

"One of the fascinating things about crewing on a dredge boat was that no matter what nationality or color crewmembers were they all got treated equally," said Eddie. "We lived together, ate together, got the exact same pay, and got along very well. Color didn't matter. It was always like that. When there was segregation on the mainland, crews aboard the dredge boats were never segregated. I always found that interesting."

During two of Eddie's years on the skipjack, he volunteered to be the cook. "The cook spent a lot of time in the warm cabin where the stove was — that was a lot better than being out there on that cold, icy deck," he said. "One day the boat was working out of Tilghman Island and I noticed that we were low on hot dogs. I couldn't understand where the supply of hot dogs went. We had no refrigeration on the boat and the food was stored in lockers in the cabin. We had plenty of hot dogs a few days before. I questioned each crew member and they all swore they had not eaten any of the hot dogs. Finally, I got off the boat and went to Miss Mary McCarty's store and bought more hot dogs. A short time later we kept finding bits and pieces of hot dogs all over the boat. We'd find them in the forpeak and in equipment lockers that were seldom used. A rat had found the hot dogs and was hiding them in strange places. Eventually, we captured the rat and had no further thefts."

Eddie worked as a crewmember on the *Martha Lewis* for seven years. "One year, during the last week of the season, we were dredging in the Choptank River and we hit two hills of oysters," said Eddie. "The first day there we caught a lot of snaps. Snaps are oysters that are very elongated and wide. Usually buyers didn't want them because they are hard to shuck, but, because it was the last week of the season, processors would buy anything. A crewmember on deck was feeling the line. He had his hand around the cable that is attached to the dredge as it rides over the bottom. When you feel a dredge that's in the mud, it's spongy, but, when you come up on oysters, the line jiggles and vibrates as it travels over them. The guy on the line told the captain, 'We're on 'em.' The wind was just right for dredging the two hills. The boat was sailing perfectly; the sails were full and we were going at just the right speed for dredging. Gene threw out buoys on either end of the lick (to mark where the oysters were located). The first couple of licks (passes) we got really small amounts of oysters. Eventually, we started getting more and more oysters. We'd get about five hundred every time we wound up the dredge. The limit in those days was 150 bushels a day and we caught 175. We caught that many by lunch time. Catching that many oysters is hard to do when dredging under sail power. That evening, when we got back into the harbor, one of the old guys on another boat told Gene, 'I knew them oysters were out there all the time.' Gene just looked at him and replied, 'If you knew they were there, why in the hell haven't you been out there and caught 'em.'"

While the *Martha* was laying at the dock in Tilghman one day, the captain chose to stay in port rather than venturing out with a storm approaching. "A lot of dredgers went out in spite of the fact that a squall was inevitable," said Eddie. "A lot of the boats that did go out were swamped by the storm."

If ice was beginning to form in the Bay, the *Martha Lewis* would travel to Solomons. "Solomons is a good ice harbor," Eddie said. "It's always one of the last places on the Chesapeake that freezes; that is probably due to the fact that most of the wind is from the west and the harbor there is wide open. Another factor that keeps the harbor open is that the state boats are in and out of there a lot. This helps keep the harbor open."

Life on the water could be dangerous. Eddie recalled that one cold March day, five crewmembers from the *Ida Mae*, a skipjack out of Deal Island, and a Smith Islander who was crewing on a boat that was gill netting, were drowned.

During his stint on the *Martha Lewis,* Somers obtained a 27-foot boat and used it for crab scraping during summers. "She was a box stern boat, built in the 1950s," said Eddie. "Dad gave me the boat. She didn't have a name on her stern. It was unusual to use a box stern (square stern) boat for scraping in the 1950s. Most crab-scraping boats had a great amount of deadrise that ran all the way aft."

Eventually, Somers bought a Deltaville (Va.)-built boat. "Her name was *Barbara Jean* and I used her for crab potting for four or five years," he continued.

Later, he bought a 38-foot boat and named it *Last One.* "I crab-potted in *Last One* for four or five more years and then bought a smaller boat that I named *Last One II. Last One II* was twenty-nine feet long. I had three hundred crab pots and the last year I crab-potted I got into a load of hair. Hair is different from SAV, it's very heavy stuff and you can hardly pull it apart. It got wound around my wheel and into my pots. It was a mess. I began to think that there must be a better way to make a living than crab potting. The boys around Smith Island tease me and tell me that getting involved with that hair was the best thing that ever happened to me because I was able to eventually get a state job."

In 1981, Eddie married a girl from Rhodes Point on Smith Island. "Shelly was in her senior year at Salisbury University working on a nursing degree," said Eddie. "She wanted to move to the mainland, so we settled in Crisfield and have been there for the last thirty years." The couple has two sons: Justin, who is twenty-six, and nineteen-year-old Alex. "Justin works as a Correctional Officer over to the Eastern Correctional Institution in Princess Anne and Alex is studying nuclear engineering at North Carolina State," Eddie explained.

In 1987, Eddie began working at the Chesapeake Bay Pilot Station in Solomons as a deckhand. He was assigned to the boats that transfer Chesapeake Bay Pilots from shore to ships. Ships are required to use Chesapeake pilots as they transverse the Bay. Pilots are captains that are highly-trained in the art and science of navigating the Bay.

"We worked seven days on and seven days off," Eddie said. "When the weather was calm, the job was fine, but when it was rough, things were much more difficult. We had to pull alongside the ship as it was traveling at fifteen knots or so. There was a lot of wash from the ship's wake and we had to fight to get close enough to reach the ladder that would be lowered down from the upper deck of the ship. Out on the deck of the pilot boat, I had to grab the ladder and hold it while the relief pilot climbed up to the deck of the ship and the pilot being relieved climbed down to our boat. It could be dangerous as the boat rolled and rocked over high waves when it was stormy or foggy."

Eddie worked at the pilot station for two years. While employed there, he earned his captain's license. Eventually, he upgraded to a 200-ton license. With that credential, Eddie was qualified to captain boats with a gross weight not exceeding two hundred tons. In 1989, Somers joined the fisheries program of the Maryland Department of Natural Resources. In June 1990, he was appointed deckhand on the *J. Millard Tawes.* A few years later, he was appointed mate and, in 1995, was named the vessel's Captain, the position he has held since that time.

While working at the Pilot Station, Eddie's wife's uncle was building his own house. "I told him I'd help him on my days off if he'd teach me about house-building," said Eddie. "The arrangement was that he didn't have to pay me; I just wanted the experience. He agreed, and I bought a book about home construction and studied it. We finished the house and I started building the house I'm living in today. A few years later I bought an old house next door and tore it down. I built a new house on the lot and sold it. It was a small rancher, nothing fancy. I made a little bit of money from that."

Somers explained that there was a house on Smith Island for sale. Located in the town of Rhodes Point, the house had been built in the 1950s and needed a lot of work. "The house had pine and oak floors and I was able to save two of the pine floors," Eddie stated. "I refinished them and they turned out nice. I spent lots of money rehabbing the place. I paid an electrician to rewire it and built a porch on. When it was finished, the house turned out really well. I sold the house and made some profit."

With the profit he made from the house, Eddie bought a piece of land on Rhodes Point that had a house trailer on it. "I bought the property a few years ago when the economy had tanked and lumber was cheap," he continued. "I bought a 24-foot outboard-powered skiff, got a loan, and started hauling materials over to Smith Island in the boat. I started building a house on the lot. I probably hauled 90% of the building materials that went into the house in my skiff."

Eddie explained that the house is a three-story affair. "I had an architect draw the plans for the house," he said. "It has a small footprint, only 20' by 16', because the lot is not very big. The house looks like a vacation home, similar to the houses at the seashore. I was going to put a cupola on top to make it look like a lighthouse, but that would have cost an extra $3,000. That'll just have to wait; maybe it'll be added later. There is an 8- by 8-foot porch on each level. The living area is on the middle floor and the bottom and top floors are where the bedrooms are."

Capt. Somers continued by explaining that, originally, he built the house to sell. He also owns a piece of land across the road and his intention was to build another house on that lot. Water and sewer is available and building permits would not be problematic to obtain.

"When I was framing up the house, I stood on the second floor and looked out," Eddie stated. "I called Shelly and told her that I didn't know if I wanted to sell the house or not. The view was breathtaking. The house faces the Chesapeake Bay and, on a clear day, I can see Smith Point Light and Point Lookout on the western side of the Bay. Then I went up to the third floor and we both looked at the view from there and agreed that we couldn't sell the house. The view is that good. The sunsets are beautiful, you can't beat it...but we may have to sell it, though. We have college tuition to pay, I don't know, we'll see."

Even though he has not lived full-time on Smith Island for many years, Eddie is fond of visiting his homeland. "I love going over there still," he said. "From my house I can walk within a hundred yards of some of the best rock fishing in the Bay. I don't even have to get in a boat to do it; we just fish right off the bank. My son has caught some pretty speckled trout in the same spot. You can't beat it. If I had to buy a place like that on the mainland, I couldn't afford it."

After retirement, Eddie would happily move back to Smith Island. "I could retire over there and be happy, but I don't know if my wife could," he stated. "She's not sure if she wants to live there full-time. If we don't move there, we may use it as a vacation home."

In his spare time, Eddie enjoys building model boats. Partially, Eddie attributes his interest in model boat-building to frequenting Lawson Tyler's boat-building shop

Skipjack model by Eddie Somers, Jr.
Courtesy of Eddie E. Somers, Jr.

in Ewell when he was a boy. "Two of my friends and I visited Lawson's shop a lot while we were growing up," he stated. "I used to think that Lawson had an ideal life. His shop was located right behind his house on the water and all he had to do to go to work was go out his back door. He built lots of sailing boats and round sterns as well as crabbing skiffs. His crabbing skiffs were used for scraping and were very fast. Back in the 1930s, they started racing them and his boats always won. One of his skiffs is on display over in Solomons, at the Calvert Maritime Museum. Lawson built boats from the early 1900s until the late 1960s. My dad had the last skiff he built in 1967."

Eddie explained that, by the time he and his friends were frequenting Tyler's shop, work was scarce and Tyler was semi-retired and had begun building model boats. "Lawson didn't seem to mind us kids hanging around his shop," he said. "In fact, he seemed to enjoy us. Watching him build those models was fascinating to me."

Eddie's father's cousin lived next-door on Smith Island and he also built boats. Eddie would often visit and watch him as he worked. "I always had an interest in it," he said.

Another influential person in Capt. Somers's life was Edward Jones. "He built model skipjacks after he retired," Eddie said. "His models were so detailed that he appeared on a morning show on network TV. His work really inspired me and I started thinking that I might want to try to build models. Eventually, I built model skipjacks, crab-scraping skiffs, and sailing skiffs. My skipjacks are based roughly on the design of the boats that Bronza Parks built. His skipjacks were beautiful; he had a good eye for boat design. It took me about six or eight months to build two model skipjacks. Of course, I only work on them part-time."

Eddie is currently in the process of building two sailing skiff models. "The design came from Howard Chappele's (a well-known yacht designer) plans, which dated back to the 1940s," he said. "Sailing skiffs are double-enders with centerboards. I actually sailed one when I was a kid.

"Two brothers who lived across the road, Homer and Lee Tyler, had a grandfather who owned a sailing skiff. It was pulled up in the marsh and one day we decided to take it for a sail. We pulled it out of the marsh, found the sails and mast, and Homer and I climbed aboard. We weren't over ten years old at the time. We didn't know anything about centerboards. We put up the sail and the boat took off. Lee was standing on the shore watching as Homer and I pushed her away from the shore. There was a strong northwest wind blowing and the boat went down the creek sideways. We couldn't make the boat go straight. When their father came home from crabbing, he explained the use of the centerboard. He went and found it, put it in the boat, and took the three of us sailing that evening. He steered with a long wooden paddle; I don't remember a rudder being attached to the boat."

Eddie's father-in-law told him a story about double-ended sailing skiffs. "The very first guy on Smith Island to have a boat with an engine in it set up a little business for himself," Eddie stated. "He'd charge 25 cents a week to tow a sailing skiff out to the crabbing grounds. My father-in-law said you could look out and see a line of skiffs going down the creek, single-file, being towed by the powerboat. In those days, the man probably made pretty good money."

Eddie also builds models of Smith Island crab-scraping boats. "They are my favorite because I remember them well," he said. "I can complete a crab-scraping skiff in about four weekends." Eddie hopes to supplement his retirement income by continuing to build models after his formal working days. "Maybe I can make enough money to go out to dinner now and then," he laughed.

Turning to the status of the Chesapeake Bay, Eddie has concerns. "Until the 1980s, crabbers never had to wash a crab pot," he said. "Now, all the boats carry pressure washers and everyday the crab pots are power-washed. The water is filthy and crabs won't go into a dirty crab pot. This change has come on fast, I don't know why. Grass beds around Tangier and Smith Islands are in pretty good shape right now. After Hurricane Agnes went through, the grasses all died, but they've bounced back…but, as the islands erode away, the grasses surrounding them are smothered.

"There are far fewer crabbers now than there used to be. There are probably 80% fewer watermen than there were in the 1970s. When I was growing up, there were seventy-eight full-time watermen living in Rhodes Point and Ewell. I'm sure that if Tylerton was included, that number would reach one hundred. If you included all the surrounding areas where watermen lived, there were a tremendous number of them out there in the Bay. Now, just a fraction of those numbers are out there. I don't know why, but the health of the Bay must be a contributing factor."

Life on Smith Island, according to Eddie, has its drawbacks. "In a lot of ways, it's a good lifestyle," he said. "But in a lot of ways, it is not. Some of the watermen who work from the island love their work. Those that do will do well. I didn't love it enough. I enjoy everything about the Smith Island lifestyle, but getting out there and actually working on the water was not what I wanted. I wasn't willing to put in twelve- and fifteen-hour days."

Eddie very much enjoys and appreciates the culture and heritage of the area. "It just interests me," he said. "I like sitting around the stores and hearing the old-timers talk about the old days. Those conversations are disappearing quickly. In Crisfield, some of that remains. Gordon's Confectionery is the last place in town where you can hear the old-timers. I still love to go there and listen to their stories.

"The communities were a whole lot closer and tighter than they are now. People knew each other and were close. It's different now. Some hoped that the condos would help the economy in Crisfield. The only thing they've done for me is raise my taxes. I'd prefer to see the old processing plants around the harbor rather than the condominiums. I do miss the old days."

Capt. Edward Somers is a delight. His warm, caring personality endears him to all. His honesty and straight-forward manner is refreshing. It is rewarding to be in his presence.

Afterword

The Chesapeake Bay has a long history of influencing those who reside along her shores. Eleven of these men have been discussed between the covers of this book. Although each man is unique, and their stories vary, the Chesapeake has branded them similarly. Each of them has a high regard and respect for the Bay. They are united in their belief that the great Chesapeake they hold so dear is critically ill and in desperate need of attention. Cautiously, they are pessimistic about the ability, and willingness, of our culture to apply the treatments necessary to affect a cure.

These are not men of science armed with knowledge gained from a multitude of studies of the Chesapeake. Instead, these are men who have years of experience interacting with the Bay. Their theories are based on common sense and a knowledge base passed down from past generations. These men understand well the many moods of the mighty Chesapeake. Because of this, the Bay has their respect and admiration. When these men talk, we should all listen intently — perhaps somewhere in their passion and desire for a cleaner Bay, the answers lie.

These are men of substance and wholesomeness. Straight-forward and honest, they tell it like it is. Characters all, some more so than others, but none is void of character. When their word is given, it can be taken to the bank. All are endowed with a great degree of sincerity. Approachable and spiritual in their beliefs about the Chesapeake and about life in general, these men are respectful and respected by those known to them. They are wonderful examples of how the human race should be. It has been a joy, and a true honor, to have interacted with them in the compilation of this book.

Two of the men mentioned on these pages (Bob Theiler and Eddie Somers) inquired about a follow-up to *Chesapeake Men: Their Stories, Their Memories*. Bob and Eddie suggested that the women of the Chesapeake should also be given a chance to tell their stories. Their advice was sound and taken seriously. *Chesapeake Women: Their Stories, Their Memories* will soon be joining its masculine counterpart and become part of the Schiffer offerings.

Individualistic, entertaining, and steadfast in their beliefs, not unlike their counterparts in "Chesapeake Men," the women selected for inclusion in "Chesapeake Women" are fascinating and unforgettable with a unique story to tell.

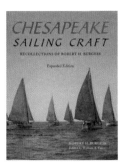

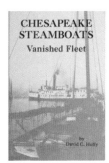

Yesterday on the Chesapeake Bay. JamesTigner. Enjoy a nostalgic view of yesteryear's Chesapeake Bay, with 466 vintage black and white and hand-tinted postcards presenting a relaxed atmosphere of beaches, riverboats, amusement parks, and fishing, from Baltimore to Norfolk. Includes a section on dating and pricing postcards.
Size: 11" x 8 1/2" • 204 color & 262 b/w photos • Price Guide • 160 pp.
ISBN: 978-0-7643-2597-7• hard cover • $39.95

Chesapeake Sailing Craft: Recollections of Robert H. Burgess. Robert H.Burgess. Edited by William A. Fox. A rare photographic record of 1925-1975 sailing craft, from log canoe to four-masted schooner. Vessels appear in all phases of their activities, including loading & unloading cargoes, under sail, in port & shipyard, details of rigging, fittings, decks, interior views, as powerboats, and as abandoned hulks.
Size: 8 1/2" x 11" • 463 b/w photos • Index • 324 pp.
ISBN: 978-0-87033-572-3• hard cover • $34.95

Pirates on the Chesapeake: Being a True History of Pirates, Picaroons, and Raiders on the Chesapeake Bay, 1610-1807. Donald G.Shomette. Pirates, picaroons, and sea rovers are pitted against the representatives of an outpost in the Chesapeake Bay region. It is a two hundred-year history that begins with the Virginia colony in 1609 and ends with the peaceful resolution of the Othello affair in 1807.
Size: 6" x 9" • 39 illustrations, 1 map • Index • 252 pp.
ISBN: 978-0-87033-607-2• soft cover • $22.95

Chesapeake Steamboats: Vanished Fleet. David C.Holly. From the first steamboat on the bay in 1813 to the last in 1963, this account relates adventures and personalities of colorful dimensions. A particular highlight is the account of the steamer Columbus, built in 1828, that burned and sank in 1850 near the mouth of the Potomac River. A theme of ghostliness runs through the pages.
Size: 6" x 9" • 18 illustrations, 8 b/w photos, 6 maps • Index • 320 pp.
ISBN: 978-0-87033-455-9• hard cover • $29.95